A PENGUIN SPECIAL

S152

The Profumo Affair: Aspects of Conservatism

WAYLAND YOUNG

WAYLAND YOUNG

THE PROFUMO AFFAIR
ASPECTS OF CONSERVATISM

PENGUIN BOOKS

Penguin Books Ltd, Harmondsworth, Middlesex
AUSTRALIA: Penguin Books Pty Ltd, 762 Whitehorse Road,
Mitcham, Victoria

—

First published 1963

—

Copyright © Wayland Young, 1963

—

Made and printed in Great Britain
by C. Nicholls & Company Ltd
Set in Monotype Times

ACKNOWLEDGEMENT

The author's warm thanks are due to Mr Robin Murray for his help in cutting the Press and in general research.

W.Y.

FOREWORD

THIS is a long pamphlet, not a book. Books should be written slowly and revised over and over again. The Profumo Affair will deserve a book in time, probably after all the protagonists are dead, certainly after all the lawsuits are over and the electric atmosphere of libel has died down.

In the meantime it seemed interesting to try and sort out, within the limited knowledge which is all that an outsider can have, even after the Denning Report, and within the cramping confines of our libel laws, and without the benefit of a transcript of the Ward trial which his publishers were refused by the Lord Chief Justice, what the Affair can teach us about sexual morals in public life, about national security, and about political mendacity. (Lays, leaks, and lies.) To do this I have had to tell some of the story again, but I have done so in my own way, emphasizing what seemed to me instructive and leaving out what did not. The story has already been well told in plain narrative by other writers. The Denning Report is not an account of the Profumo Affair, it is part of it. The purpose of the present pamphlet is to talk round and about the Affair as a whole and draw conclusions about how politics are carried on, how they ought to be carried on, and the relation between the *is* and the *ought*.

Many people were astonished by the Profumo Affair, some by what happened, others by the convulsive public reaction, and there is probably room for a good few pamphlets yet, before all that is worth saying about it has been said. The Affair illuminated several issues of real importance (only the most dedicated supporters of the Macmillan Government could claim they were trivial), and the more is thought and written about these issues the less likely does it become that the general political atmosphere will permit anything like this summer's events to recur.

October 1963   Wayland Young

THE first the British public heard of the Profumo Affair was in July 1962, eight months before it knew it had heard of it. There was a feature in *Queen* called 'Sentences I'd like to hear the end of . . .'. One of these ran: '. . . called in M.I.5 because every time the chauffeur-driven Zis drew up at her *front* door, out of the *back* door into a chauffeur-driven Humber slipped . . .'. The feature was a collection of in-group innuendo; it consisted entirely of such half-sentences as these. Some of them related to scandals and situations already known to Fleet Street and Westminster (there are a few such at any time) and some of them were fanciful constructions of greater or less charm. Not more than a few hundred people would have taken all the points, and the great majority of the British people would not have taken any.

The particular one about the Zis and the Humber came initially from Stephen Ward, osteopath, portrait draughtsman, procurer, and suicide; and the fact that it did so is of an importance which will appear later. She with the doors was Christine Keeler, then aged nineteen. The two visitors were the Rt Hon. John Profumo, Secretary of State for War, and Commander Yevgeny Ivanov, Assistant Soviet Naval Attaché in London. The situation referred to had occurred about a year previously, in 1961; Stephen Ward, in telling the story to his friends, and in evidence at his trial in 1963, maintained he had informed the Security Service of it in 1961.

How many scandalous situations – or rather how many situations which would scandalize most people if they knew about them – remain for ever unknown, and thus not scandalous, because nobody happens to turn up and fire a pistol at a front door? A whole chain of events, compound of chance and character, brought the Profumo Affair to light; the first of these was the Edgecombe affray. On 14 December 1962 a young West Indian called Johnny Edgecombe turned up in a hired car at the door of a flat in Wimpole Mews, a quiet doctorish part of central London, and fired a number of shots at the window and the door lock. Inside were two girls called Christine Keeler and Marilyn, or Mandy, Rice-Davies. The flat belonged to Dr Stephen Ward, who was round the corner in his consulting-room at the time. They telephoned to him, and he called the police. Edgecombe ran back to his car and told the driver to drive him away. Later he was arrested.

Who were the girls, who was Ward, who was Edgecombe? 'Models', 'an osteopath', 'a West Indian'. The mass circulation papers are for ever full of stories about people with generic titles like these, and the general reader usually feels 'O yes; the under-world'. Or perhaps 'O yes, people trying to make an under-worldish story out of some people who really are just models or osteopaths or West Indians'. The police began to find out more about them (though they knew a good deal already) and several prominent politicians and others must have begun to look over their shoulders at this time.

On 8 March 1963 a publication, if indeed it could be called that, so small was its circulation, entitled *Westminster Confidential* gave for the first time in semi-public form the rough outlines of the situation. It wrote, and Lord Denning later quoted it in his famous report:

One of the choicest bits in their stories [that is, two girls who had started selling their stories to the newspapers] was a letter, apparently signed 'Jock', on the stationery of the Secretary for W + r. The allegation by this girl was that not only was this Minister, who has a famous actress as his wife, her client, but also the Soviet military attaché, apparently a Colonel Ivanov. The famous actress-wife, of course, would sue for divorce, the scandal ran. Who was using the call-girl to 'milk' whom of information – the W + r Secretary or the Soviet military attaché? – ran the minds of those primarily interested in security.

But nothing came into the public Press until 14 March, when Edgecombe came up for trial at the Old Bailey. The scandal then began in earnest.

Christine Keeler was not there; she had skipped. Mandy Rice-Davies was, and gave evidence; but there was already a feeling that Christine Keeler was the more significant of the two. She was three years older; Mandy Rice-Davies was actually a minor; only eighteen. The main prosecution witness was absent, but the prosecution did not ask for a postponement of the trial until she could be found. They asked for it to go on. Edgecombe was tried not only for shooting at the missing witness, but also for wounding his successor in her affections, another coloured man called Lucky Gordon; an episode which had taken place in her presence. He was found not guilty of this, or of the major charge – attempting to murder Christine Keeler; and found guilty only of a minor one – possessing a firearm with intent to endanger life. After the verdict, the court learned that he already had convictions for theft, possession of drugs, and 'living on immoral earnings'. He got seven years. He had done it because she had lived with him for a time, and he wanted her back, or dead; at any rate he wanted a change from life without her (see p. 89 below).

The papers said that Christine Keeler had many rich and famous friends, and quoted Stephen Ward to the effect that he had 'about half the cabinet' among his patients. They gave something of Christine Keeler's life story. Her parents lived in the Western suburbs of London, and she had worked in a night club when she first came to the city. The look of the people began to be familiar. Christine Keeler had long rust-coloured hair which came out black in the photographs, straight and fine. A clear-featured, beautiful face, but unpleasantly precise lips. The earlier photographs showed a pert, cheap kid; the later ones a fleshing-out with thought and feeling but also something empty, unlively. The body compact, lithe, and fertile-looking; the European man's dream, not the American's. Mandy Rice-Davies with masses of golden hair all over the place, face all alight with humour and perhaps defenceless courage; romanesque brows, duckling nose, little round head on a long neck, and bearing erect like a Latin girl. Stephen Ward, in well-preserved middle age; high-nosed, self-satisfied look, something haughty about him, but prompt, apt, neat.

The Press was in an unusually jumpy frame of mind at this time. An Admiralty clerk called Vassall had recently been convicted of spying for the Soviet Union; the Russians had blackmailed him into it by getting him to a homosexual party when he was serving in the British Embassy in Moscow, and photographing him there. Some of the papers later alleged he had been known as a homosexual by his colleagues for years

11

and had been protected by higher-up queers. A Tribunal of Inquiry was set up by the Government, and two reporters refused to tell it where they got their information. The Tribunal used its quasi-judicial powers and sent them to prison. They were still in prison at the time of the Profumo Affair, and journalists were divided about whether they had been right to refuse to speak, as well as full of a new sense of caution for themselves.

At this time, then, every journalist on the national Press, as well as almost every politically active person and most politically conscious people in the country, had heard the story that Christine Keeler had had affairs, perhaps simultaneously, with both Profumo and Ivanov. Most of them, on the basis of common sense and experience, believed the story. But they did not jump into print.

They had recourse instead to the technique of meaningful juxtaposition. On 15 March and succeeding days, the mass circulation papers ran the Edgecombe story on their front page close to a story about discontent in parts of the Brigade of Guards, where a quasi-mutinous situation existed, and Mr Profumo's plans for putting it right. The *Express* and the *Herald* made quite obvious juxtapositions and the *Daily Mail* devoted five out of six front page columns to the operation. Left to right it ran:

(1) 'Comment' on the refusal of the Government to remit the sentences of the two reporters imprisoned by the Vassal Tribunal; (2) 'Guards Inquiry; Something wrong at Pirbright, says Minister'; (3) 'Model in shooting case vanishes.', with a picture of Christine Keeler; (4) (an extraneous story;) (5) 'New evidence about the imprisoned reporters'; and (6) 'Profumo denial; I am not resigning' with a picture of Mr and Mrs Profumo side by side. Five days later the *Mirror* used the technique: 'Now police start hunt for the "lost" model', with a fairly undressed picture of Christine Keeler, next to: 'Walk-out threat by Guards' wives: problem for War Office'.

The *Sunday Pictorial* ran an interview with Stephen Ward in which a new leg was added to the legend. Among those he said had sat for him to have their portraits drawn were quite a number of royals: Prince Philip, Princess Marina (the dowager Duchess of Kent), the present Duke and Duchess of Kent, and Lord

Snowdon. Also 'men like' Paul Getty (oil millionaire), Duncan Sandys (at that time Secretary of State for Commonwealth and Colonial Affairs), Douglas Fairbanks (smart set), and Nubar Gulbenkian (oil millionaire). Stephen Ward, or more probably the journalist who interviewed him, also began to bring the shape of Christine Keeler's life into focus:

For instance, there was that occasion in Paris when she hi-jacked her boy-friend's car and gaily drove down to the South of France in it with another girl.
A wild escapade that could have got her into very serious trouble with the French police.
But, as always happened with Christine – the dear charming beautiful girl that she is – there was always someone to help her.
This time it was a senior naval officer of the American Fleet who sorted out her problems and gave her the money to fly back home.
It occurs to me that she would be happier today if her friends had not been quite so helpful.
Now it looks as though somebody – no doubt a loyal friend – has spirited her away.

The interview also said that Ivanov had been a friend of Ward's and Christine Keeler's, and was full of verbiage about how readily wicked tongues will mock the word 'friendship'.

From then on, the affair gathered pace. Two days later the Labour M.P. Marcus Lipton tabled a parliamentary question to the Home Secretary asking why the police had not appeared to put themselves out to find the principal prosecution witness in a case of attempted murder, but withdrew it the next day because Edgecombe's appeal against his sentence brought the matter once again *sub judice*. Two days later again, another Labour M.P., Alice Bacon, saw her question rejected on the grounds that the Home Secretary was not responsible for the conduct of prosecutions. Parliament began to boil.

Fleet Street boiled too. The Editor of *The Times*, still, as it happened, thinking about the last scandal, had left his office for a few days, and returned with a long selection of letters about the Vassall Tribunal, and a burning leader called 'It *is* Happening Here'.

The letters almost all attacked the Press for muck-raking and malice; the leader was a dignified cry of alarm against the ostrich

13

attitude of 'It can't happen here'. It maintained that the letters showed that the British people had already lost confidence in their Press, and that the Press was thereby becoming incapable of being the watchdog of freedom; abuses could henceforth flourish unchecked. The *Daily Mirror*, foremost among those usually attacked by *The Times* and the other quality papers for alleged muck-raking, reprinted the leader *in extenso* the next day, expressing breathless agreement.

At this stage, such was the constipation in Fleet Street as a result of the imprisonment of the two Vassall case reporters, the general newspaper reader had very little idea of what was really happening. The spectacle of a small number of people who are fully informed bursting to give some news to a large number of people who know nothing of it but ought to, and not daring to, was in one way alarming, in another comic. *Private Eye*, a fortnightly born only the year before and already established as the bravest, and often the most accurate, organ of opinion in the British Press, summed up the situation as follows on 22 March:

IDLE TALK
Reveals
Lunchtime O'Booze
Mr Silas Jones, a West Indian immigrant of no fixed abode, was today sentenced at the Old Bailey to twenty-four years' Preventive Detention for being in possession of an offensive water pistol.

The chief 'witness' in the case, gay fun-loving Miss Gaye Funloving, a twenty-one-year-old 'model', was not actually present in Court. She has, in fact, disappeared. It is believed that normally, in cases of this type, a Warrant is issued for the arrest of the missing witness.

'PARTIES'
One of Miss Funloving's close 'friends', Dr Spook of Harley Street, revealed last night that he could add nothing to what had already been insinuated.

Dr Spook is believed to have 'more than half the Cabinet on his list of patients'. He also has a 'weekend' cottage on the Berkshire estate of Lord —, and is believed to have attended many 'parties' in the neighbourhood.

Among those it is believed have also attended 'parties' of this type are Mr Vladimir Bolokhov, the well-known Soviet spy attached to the Russian Embassy, and a well-known Cabinet Minister.

Mr James Montesi, a well-known Cabinet Minister, was last night reported to have proffered his 'resignation' to the Prime Minister, on 'personal grounds'.

It is alleged that the Prime Minister refused to accept his alleged 'resignation'. Mr Montesi today denied the allegations that he had ever allegedly offered his alleged 'resignation' to the alleged 'Prime Minister'.

On the evening of the day this story appeared, and it was the fullest yet, the scandal broke in earnest in the House of Commons. The man who finally took the bull by the horns was the Labour member George Wigg. In the big debate later on, in June, he said: 'I'm not going to wear a surplice because if I did, my puttees would soon show.' Wigg, one of the most individual members of a party of individualists, rose from the ranks to become a colonel in the British Army during the Second World War, and the love of his life has always been the Army. He speaks regularly on Army affairs in the Commons, and devotes the most minute and intensive study to all military matters. Because of this he gets to know successive Secretaries of State for War more intimately, in the political sense, than many of his colleagues. He had often before expressed doubts of Profumo's probity; there had been a particularly heated and detailed row between the Conservative Minister and the Labour Back-bencher a year earlier when British troops had been sent in battle order to protect Kuwait from a possible Iraqi attack. Some of them succumbed to heat stroke. Wigg suspected Profumo of concealing how many, and considerable tension existed between the two men.

At around midnight, when the House of Commons was still debating the two reporters imprisoned by the Vassall Tribunal, Wigg said: 'There is not an Hon. Member in the House, nor a journalist in the Press Gallery, nor do I believe there is a person in the Public Gallery who in the last few days has not heard rumour upon rumour involving a member of the Government Front Bench. The Press has got as near as it can – it has shown itself willing to wound but afraid to strike. This all comes about because of the Vassall Tribunal. In actual fact, these great Press Lords, these men who control great instruments of public

15

opinion and of power, do not have the guts to discharge the duty that they are now claiming for themselves.

'That being the case, I rightly use the privilege of the House of Commons – that is what it is given to me for – to ask the Home Secretary, who is the senior member of the Government on the Treasury Bench now, to go to the Dispatch Box – he knows that the rumour to which I refer relates to Miss Christine Keeler and Miss Davies and a shooting by a West Indian – and, on behalf of the Government, categorically deny the truth of these rumours. On the other hand, if there is anything in them, I urge him to ask the Prime Minister to do what was not done in the Vassall case – set up a Select Committee so that these things can be dissipated, and the honour of the Minister concerned freed from the imputations and innuendoes that are being spread at the present time.'

He was backed up by Richard Crossman, who pointed out how much more would probably appear in the foreign Press than in the home Press, and by Barbara Castle, who inquired whether the disappearance of Christine Keeler might not suggest a 'perversion of justice'. Members on the Government side tried to induce the three Labour members to be more specific about the rumours, but they would not be. They were also attacked from their own side by Reginald Paget, another spokesman on military affairs who, unlike Wigg, comes from one of the longest-established families of the English squirearchy. 'I have seen it stated nowhere before this evening,' he said; and moreover: 'What do these rumours amount to? They amount to the fact that a Minister is said to be acquainted with a very pretty girl. I should have thought that was a matter for congratulation rather than inquiry.' Later events hardly justified such bluff worldliness.

The last word from the Government that night was from Henry Brooke, the Home Secretary, who said: 'I do not propose to comment on rumours which have been raised under the cloak of privilege and safe from any action at law. Mr Wigg and Mrs Castle should seek other means of making these insinuations if they are prepared to substantiate them.'

Profumo was not in the House that night, but when the debate ended his colleagues got him out of bed. What happened

16

then only became known later, and only in part. The next public move was a personal statement by Profumo.

The Personal Statement is a parliamentary device whereby a member, traditionally a Back-bench member but in recent years increasingly Ministers too, can get up, interrupting a debate, and make a point of a personal nature. It is used to correct a mistake made the day before, to apologize for offence given, to clarify a personal interest, or, indeed, to deny a rumour. It is a part of the complex and largely unwritten procedure of the House of Commons that members are not questioned after personal statements; they make them, and that is that. They are thus, by long custom, occasions for a special degree of truthfulness. It is, as it is in all democratic assemblies, supposed that no one will ever lie in the House of Commons. Indeed, if a member is detected in a flagrant lie at any point in the business of the House, his career will suffer considerably. But at normal times there is a certain latitude, especially for Ministers. It is unparliamentary to accuse a member of lying, but one may traditionally accuse him of a 'terminological inexactitude'. (The phrase, like so many others, is usually attributed to Sir Winston Churchill.)

But in a personal statement, because he cannot be questioned about it, a member is held to be quite extraordinarily bound to tell the truth. In a sense, this piece of machinery only exists at all because of the felt need for special interludes of superior veracity.

At eleven o'clock on the morning after the three Labour Members had asked for an inquiry or a statement, they were answered in full measure. Profumo sat on the front bench between the Prime Minister and Iain Macleod, the Leader of the House. Mrs Profumo was in the Stranger's Gallery. Thus supported by the apparatus of credibility, he rose and spoke as follows:

'I understand that my name has been connected with the rumours about the disappearance of Miss Keeler.

'I would like to take this opportunity of making a personal statement about these matters.

'I last saw Miss Keeler in December 1961, and I have not seen her since. I have no idea where she is now. Any suggestion that

17

I was in any way connected with or responsible for her absence from the trial at the Old Bailey is wholly and completely untrue.

'My wife and I first met Miss Keeler at a house party in July 1961, at Cliveden. Among a number of people there was Dr Stephen Ward, whom we already knew slightly, and a Mr Ivanov, who was an attaché at the Russian Embassy.

'The only other occasion that my wife or I met Mr Ivanov was for a moment at the official reception for Major Gagarin at the Soviet Embassy.

'My wife and I had a standing invitation to visit Dr Ward.

'Between July and December 1961, I met Miss Keeler on about half-a-dozen occasions at Dr Ward's flat, when I called to see him and his friends. Miss Keeler and I were on friendly terms. There was no impropriety whatsoever in my acquaintanceship with Miss Keeler.

'Mr Speaker, I have made this personal statement because of what was said in the House last evening by the three Hon. Members, and which, of course, was protected by privilege. I shall not hesitate to issue writs for libel and slander if scandalous allegations are made or repeated outside the House.'

Mr and Mrs Profumo then went to the races and got photographed in the company of the Queen Mother.

The heavy emphasis on 'my wife and I', the presence of Mrs Profumo (who, under the name of Valerie Hobson, had been, before her marriage, a celebrated actress), the mute corroboration of the Prime Minister and the Leader of the House, and the curt, manly threat of libel actions if the skulking accusers would cast aside the shield of parliamentary privilege, all these carried conviction to many people. Indeed, most of the statement, as far as is yet known at the time I write, was true. But, unless one is to permit an unusual interpretation of the word *impropriety*, the assertion that there had been none in his relation with Christine Keeler was a lie.

The Press reaction varied, but was mainly on the reserved side. The *Herald* said the statement could not 'in itself end the uneasiness in the country and in Parliament over the case'. *The Times* complained of delay in facing up to the rumour, and 'relieving the mounting tension'. It coolly avoided saying whether it believed Profumo or not. The *Guardian*, perhaps because it was edited from Manchester, whither the voice of authority carries louder than the sometimes more truthful mutter of metropolitan gossip, believed with alacrity. 'Newspapers are suspicious of official denials. They have learned by hard experience. Even so, only the most compelling evidence to the contrary could warrant any suspicion now, after such explicit statements from Mr Profumo, that his words are not the plain truth. Unless anyone has such evidence, it would be grossly unjust not to accept his words at their face value. They ought to end the talk.'

In Spain, where she had at last been found by the Press, Christine Keeler said: 'I have nothing to be ashamed of; I know that now.' In London Stephen Ward, refusing to be interviewed but insisting on making a 'statement' too, said on television that Profumo had told the truth about Christine Keeler. He accepted a fee of five pounds for his appearance.

Private Eye printed on its front cover a photograph of Profumo sitting on a bed with a balloon saying: 'And if Private Eye prints a picture of me on a bed, I'll sue them.'

AFFAIRS, or big political scandals, often have a slow movement, a sort of lull, after the alarming opening. During April and May the time bomb ticked away, audible to all except, as he later assured the world, the Prime Minister. The public appetite for sexual scandal was satisfied for a time by the divorce of the Duke of Argyll from his third Duchess, which was said to be the most expensive suit in British history (£50,000). Who was the man in the photographs taken with a polaroid camera doing something with the Duchess which, the judge said, would be of more interest to a woman with a sexual perversion than to a man with a sexual perversion, whose head did not show, and who, according to 'an expert' was not the Duke? And why should the Duke have produced the photographs at a party and laughed about them? If, as was widely believed, the man without the head was another Minister (Lord Hailsham later said it wasn't him) then here was another time bomb.

The name of Lord Astor began to crop up more frequently; so far it was only known that Stephen Ward rented a cottage from him; the riverside *cottage orné* under Cliveden Woods which generations have admired from boats and from the opposite towpath. (At different times other cottages at Cliveden had been let to various in-group luminaries, including Hugh Frazer, the Secretary of State for Air.) Somebody broke into Lord Astor's London house, opened all the mail that was waiting for him, and took away one letter. The episode was never explained.

On the late Saturday television show *That Was The Week That Was*, Christine Keeler, impersonated by Millicent Martin, was knocked down to the highest newspaper bidder. In a mainly laudatory article about the first season of this show the *Observer*, edited by Lord Astor's brother David Astor, blamed it only for 'the stoning of Miss Keeler'.

Christine Keeler herself turned up from Spain and went to the Old Bailey, where she forfeited the £40 recognizance she had entered into as a witness for the Edgecombe trial. It was said on her behalf that she had several times telephoned the police to ask when the trial would be, and they had told her that it was delayed because another witness had had a heart attack. She therefore thought it safe to go to Spain. As she left the Old Bailey a coloured film extra called Aloysius, or Lucky, Gordon tried to break through a police cordon and speak to her. He was frogmarched away by the police.

Profumo, executing the threat he had made in the Commons, commenced proceedings for libel against *Paris Match* and *Tempo Illustrato*. He accepted £50 from the last in an out-of-court settlement, and gave it to an Army charity.

Just after midnight, on 18 April, there occurred the second of the two alleged attacks on Christine Keeler by coloured men which gave rise to such baffling trials. She told the police that as she was leaving the flat of a friend called Paula Hamilton-Marshall, where she had been spending the evening, Gordon, who had been waiting outside, punched her, knocked her down, and kicked her on the ground. Gordon was arrested, and at the committal proceedings the next day the police opposed bail, saying there was reason to believe he would try to intimidate witnesses.

Mandy Rice-Davies, on her way to Majorca to marry a young Spanish nobleman who was studying law, was arrested at London Airport and stood trial on 24 April for having a forged driving licence, and related offences. She had had it for a Jaguar given her on her seventeenth birthday by a property millionaire called Peter Rachman, now dead, who had been keeping her. He had also given her mink, money, jewels, etc. She was fined £42, and a man paid it for her. The court was told that she had come to London from Birmingham on a five-day trip as 'Miss Austin', paid for by the motor concern, and had been garlanded beauty queen at the Earls Court Motor Show. She had been fifteen. She had got a job at a night club called the Cabaret Club, where Christine Keeler had also worked. Rachman set her up. And died. She was broke.

She cut more of a dash than Christine Keeler. 'All the laws in this country are stupid anyhow,' she was supposed to have said when she was arrested, and 'I think men are fascinating. I can twist them round my little finger.' Some heavy moralizing

21

began in the Press, led by Godfrey Winn, the unmarried champion of respectable womanhood.

While Mandy Rice-Davies was in Holloway Gaol awaiting trial, the police questioned her about a 'call-girl ring', and a man began to be mentioned who charged £100 a night for his girls.

Meanwhile the Press kept the pot boiling by publishing a photograph of Mr and Mrs Profumo singing 'Drink to me only with thine eyes' to some elderly Tory women in his constituency. The *Mail* headlined it: 'Tory Party in Perfect Harmony'. *Private Eye* wrote: 'The late Mr Macmillan's posthumous announcement that he intends to stay on as Leader of the Conservative Party has undoubtedly come as a great tonic to Conservative Party Workers.'

Later in May it was announced that Christine Keeler was to play the part of herself in a film. Publicity brochures were handed out containing photographs of her with nothing on. John Trevelyan, the Secretary of the British Board of Film Censors, a body organized by the cinema industry itself and having no statutory power, declared that the film would not be in the public interest. The promoters said they would make it abroad. Christine Keeler later went so far as to apply for membership of Equity, the actors' trade union, which she would need if the film were to be made in England; she was not admitted.

Towards the end of May a crisis began to brew up. The Press reported that Stephen Ward had written to the Home Secretary, and quoted him: 'I laid before the Home Secretary certain facts regarding the true relationship between Mr Profumo and Miss Keeler; facts which I had hitherto taken steps to conceal, both in the interest of Mr Profumo and of the Government.' The full contents of his letter were known at once to the Press but prudence still prevailed in Fleet Street. Ben Parkin, Member of Parliament for North Paddington, put down a parliamentary question asking the Home Secretary about the letter. Paddington had succeeded Soho as the capital of the British Underworld during the last three or four years; Mr Parkin had spoken several times in the Commons showing a wide and by no means superficial knowledge and understanding of prostitution and racketeering of various sorts. But the next day he withdrew his question. By now the matter was under central direction in the Labour Party, and the leadership was not going to fire till it saw the whites of their eyes.

Johnny Edgecombe appealed against his conviction; evidence was given for him that Christine Keeler had written him a friendly letter in prison. But the appeal was dismissed.

On 30 May, James Chuter Ede, an elder statesman of the Labour Party who had been Home Secretary in the Government of 1945–51, and Ben Parkin again put down questions about Ward's letter. It was announced they would be answered three weeks later, but by then they had been overtaken by events.

Meanwhile, Lucky Gordon came up for trial at the Old Bailey. He was defended by a coloured counsel provided for him under the Legal Aid Scheme. Gordon's story was that Christine Keeler had been carrying his baby when she went off to Spain, and that he had been trying desperately to get in touch with her since her return. The night she was leaving Paula Hamilton-Marshall's flat she had fallen over her own suitcase, and that was how she had got the cuts and bruises, not from his having beaten her up. Christine Keeler hotly denied the pregnancy, but the judge would not allow a doctor to answer questions about it put by the defence. Gordon later claimed he had got V.D. from her, and her outcry of denial was such that she was led from the court. The trial became somewhat confused when Gordon decided to fire his counsel and solicitor, and look after himself. He demanded a long list of witnesses, including Profumo and Stephen Ward, but the judge ordered two only to be sought: men called Commacchio, and Truello Fenton, who, Gordon said, had been in the flat when Christine Keeler came out. (She said there had been only herself, her friend Paula, Paula's brother, and a housekeeper called Olive Booker.) These men the police could not find, although it later appeared that Commacchio was on remand and awaiting trial at that very time.

Christine Keeler maintained that she had never met Gordon except under his threat, though she admitted having once paid a £5 fine for him. A letter which defence counsel suggested was a friendly one from her to him was produced, but was not allowed to be read out, after the judge and both counsel had retired to consult about it in private.

Gordon's account of how he met Christine Keeler in the first place was that she had been sent by Stephen Ward to find a coloured girl for a foursome and that he had in fact found her a coloured girl. So much she admitted.

The judge summed up in a hanging mood, saying that the wild charges made by Gordon against all and sundry were utterly unjustified, and he was convicted. It turned out that he had had three convictions for violence in the preceding six years, and the judge told him that he regretted that the present law, which gives an immigrant security after five years, would not allow him to deport him. He sentenced him to three years. As Gordon left the court he turned to Christine Keeler and said: 'You'll see.'

Six weeks later the Lord Chief Justice, having heard some new evidence which was not made public, upset the verdict and released him.

But already on the second day of the trial the whole grumbling, menacing mess of happenings and rumours of happenings had been lifted to the level of a duly constituted scandal by the resignation of the Secretary of State for War.

Mr and Mrs Profumo had gone on holiday to Venice, but cut it short three days later. On 5 June his letter of resignation was published. He wrote:

Dear Prime Minister,

You will recollect that on 22 March, following certain allegations made in Parliament, I made a personal statement.

At that time rumour had charged me with assisting in the disappearance of a witness and with being involved in some possible breach of security.

So serious were these charges that I allowed myself to think that my personal association with that witness, which had also been the subject of rumour, was by comparison of minor importance only.

In my statement I said that there had been no impropriety in this association. To my very deep regret I have to admit that this was not true, and that I misled you, and my colleagues, and the House.

I ask you to understand that I did this to protect, as I thought, my wife and family, who were equally misled, as were my professional advisers.

I have come to realize that, by this deception, I have been guilty of a grave misdemeanour and despite the fact that there is no truth whatever in the other charges, I cannot remain a member of your Administration, nor of the House of Commons.

I cannot tell you of my deep remorse for the embarrassment I have caused to you, to my colleagues in the Government, to my constituents, and to the Party which I have served for the past twenty-five years.

Yours sincerely,
JACK PROFUMO

And the Prime Minister replied:

Dear Profumo,

The contents of your letter of 4 June have been communicated to me, and I have heard them with deep regret. This is a great tragedy for you, your family, and your friends. Nevertheless, I am sure you will understand that in the circumstances, I have no alternative but to advise the Queen to accept your resignation.

Yours very sincerely,
HAROLD MACMILLAN

The contents had had to be communicated to the Prime Minister because he was on holiday in Scotland. He stayed there and, for once perhaps overdoing his famous unflappability, went on a day-trip to Iona with his wife.

The world did not notice that Profumo continued to maintain that he had not whisked Christine Keeler out of the country at the time of the Edgecombe trial, and that he had not broken security: it noticed only that he had lied about the 'impropriety'. *The Times* wrote tartly:

There can be few more lamentable documents in British political history than Mr Profumo's letter of resignation. In his reply the Prime Minister says: 'This is a great tragedy for you, your family, and your friends.' It is also a great tragedy for the probity of public life in Britain.

The *Daily Mail* wrote hopefully:

He will cease to hold office as Secretary for War, will lose his seat as an M.P., and retire into obscurity. Such is the price demanded of one who swerves from the high standards of integrity which still, fortunately, rule the public life of this country.

The *Sketch* said: 'The truth is that the fight of newspapers for liberty is your fight.' The Editor of *The Times* used a public luncheon and Cecil King, who controls the *Mirror* Group, a television interview to say that the Press didn't publish half enough. The *Herald* called for a Select Committee of Parliament to pursue the matter. The *Guardian*, once again docile, said: 'It would be as well if the Profumo disaster could be allowed to sink as quickly as possible into oblivion' and added, as an uncomfortable afterthought: 'security permitting'. The *Daily Mirror* probably came closest to reflecting the view of the decent men and women busy with their own lives who make up the majority of the people when it wrote:

There can be nothing but pity for a suave but tarnished politician who has to admit – in a letter to his Prime Minister – that he is guilty of lying, of misleading, of deception, and of a grave misdemeanour. The words of the confession were chosen by Profumo himself.

God knows, he was never a good Minister: it seems now that he is not a very important man. But there is guilt in many a human heart, and skeletons in many cupboards.

The question is:

WHAT THE HELL IS GOING ON IN THIS COUNTRY?

Mandy Rice-Davies said: 'He did no more than any man would do, given half a chance.' And away in Ottawa Harold Wilson, the recently elected leader of the Labour Party, said: 'A Transport House official phoned to ask me what he was to say about the affair.

'I told him: "No comment – in glorious technicolor." And that's what I'm telling you: No comment – in wide-screen.'

The sharpening of knives could hardly have sounded more menacing.

The Press had indeed been operating under special difficulties during those months, but there still seemed much justification for the neat *tu quoque* set up by *Private Eye*:

Mr Lunchtime O'Booze, the well-known reporter and hack, has resigned his office as Chief Scandalmonger in the biggest sensation Fleet Street has known for years. In a letter to his proprietor, Lord Gnome, he states:

'I realize now that I can no longer continue in my post. I made an unholy mess over the Vassall Tribunal by making up a whole lot of wrong facts and now the Profumo affair, which I knew about all along, has shown me up as a weak-kneed coward.'

Mr O'Booze admitted that he had lied to the British public about the letter which Dr Stephen Ward recently sent to the Home Secretary. In his recent articles on the subject he had claimed that the letter was, in fact, on 'an undisclosed matter'. He now admitted that he knew all about the contents of the letter.

'I blamed the laws of libel at the time,' he confessed, 'but although I have recently been posing as a fearless upholder of morality and the freedom of the Press, I now admit that I was just scared of what the Government might do.

'I have in fact known the truth ever since Mr Profumo first told his pack of lies in the Commons, and I have tried to blame my evasion on the laws of libel.

'I now realize that I was gravely mistaken in so misleading the public, and I have reluctantly proffered my resignation to Lord Gnome.'

In a letter to Mr O'Booze, Lord Gnome replied:

'Thank you for your resignation, which I reluctantly accept.

'Of course, I too have known about the facts all along and have not done anything about them either. As you may remember, when this matter first came up in March, I advised you not to print anything in my paper because it was obviously a trifle dodgy, and because I thought we could get away with it. Now that Mr Profumo has confessed all, I realize that you were quite wrong not to do your duty as a journalist and print the facts as you knew them.

GNOME'

THE *Economist*, which kept its head rather well in the next few weeks, wrote: 'Mr Profumo's properly forced resignation is game, set, and match to the popular Press. The floodgates to a self-righteous scurrility have thereby been opened in precisely the wrong place. Nobody can be sure of the ultimate effects on Press, politicians, and the whole tenor of public life.'

The outline of the matter so far now began to be clear. A few months earlier, when the homosexual spy Vassall was found out and imprisoned, the mass Press, having apparently nothing better to do, had hit on the idea of insinuating that a junior minister called Galbraith, the Civil Lord of the Admiralty, was probably queer too and had protected Vassall. The Prime Minister had panicked, and accepted Galbraith's resignation. For weeks the papers had been full of pettifogging discussions whether a minister ought to write to his clerk as 'Dear Mr Vassall', or 'Dear Vassall', or 'Dear Sir', or perhaps just 'Vassall', until the pompous great Tribunal set up to inquire into it all had declared Galbraith perfectly innocent. He was shortly given another ministerial job and everybody shrugged.

But the episode had evidently left its mark on both Prime Minister and Press barons. Then, when the Press began to go gunning for Profumo, it seems likely that the Prime Minister made the mistake of his life and decided he wouldn't let them smell blood twice running. He shut his eyes and his ears, and battened down. It also seemed, from the kid gloves with which they had handled the affair, that the Press were still smarting from their discomfiture over Galbraith. But this time the prey was valid.

John Freeman, editor of the *New Statesman*, said on television that he had known the truth all along, but had not printed it because his paper could not afford the threatened libel action. The *Sunday Mirror* (as the *Sunday Pictorial* had now become) was less forthright. It published a letter from Profumo to Christine Keeler, beginning 'Darling' and ending 'Love J' which she had given them five months before, and wrote:

But for two very sound reasons the Editor of the *Sunday Pictorial* decided at the time not to publish the letter or to publish Christine Keeler's story:

(1) The Editor was not satisfied that this letter constituted evidence of any substantial nature. It was effusive but not conclusive. (2) Publication of the letter might have ruined the public career of a minister on 'evidence' from a young woman who clearly would not have produced the letter if Mr Profumo's interests were uppermost in her consideration.

Macleod, the Leader of the House of Commons, and one of the joint chairmen of the Conservative Party, said in Washington that the resignation of Profumo had come as a 'complete surprise' to him. Lord Poole, the other joint Chairman of the Party, who came increasingly into the limelight in these days, said that the affair had 'extremely serious implications and can only make the task of myself and those who are the leaders of the Conservative Party more difficult'. Harold Wilson, back from America, said it was not an issue of personal morality; the Labour Party wanted a debate in Parliament about the security aspect. John Hare, the Minister of Labour, who had earlier told George Wigg that he had not, as Wigg feared, lent his car to Profumo to take Christine Keeler out driving in, said this had been a lapse of memory; he had. Wigg said: 'I accept that. When Mr Hare told me a few weeks ago that he had no recollection of lending Mr Profumo the car, I accepted that as well.'

Stephen Ward, walking, in order to spare some friends the embarrassment of his being arrested at their house, in the streets of North Harrow, was arrested, and charged with living on the earnings of prostitution. But not before he had told the Press that he had informed the Security Service of Profumo's liaison with Christine Keeler in 1961.

Peregrine Worsthorne, columnist in the *Sunday Telegraph*, wrote that 'conservatives can survive bad measures, but not bad men and bad measures'. There began to be talk in the Press of the precedent of 1940, which was the last time a Prime Minister had been driven out of office by the open revolt of his own party in the House of Commons.

Various newspapers had for some time been picking up Christine Keeler's story and dropping it again; outbidding one

29

another, getting cold feet, finding comfort where caution and conscience joined together and discomfort where they conflicted. The *News of the World* happened to have the rights at the time of Profumo's resignation; the price had been £23,000. There was now no bar to publication, and they published. At the top of the page Christine Keeler sat naked on a small chair. (The *Sunday Mirror* the same day had her straddling it; possibly the most erotic photograph ever in the British Press.) There was a small inset of Profumo looking beaten and miserable. She wrote, in the *faux naïf* style of the ghost provided for her, that one night, as she and Stephen Ward had been swimming in the pool at Cliveden, he had thrown her bathing costume away and lo and behold! there were Lord Astor and Profumo strolling down to the pool after dinner.

But worse was to come. There were more voices – and in came the remainder of Bill's dinner guests. Including his wife, the former top model Bronwen Pugh – and of course Valerie Hobson, Jack's wife.

I can hear her saying it now – words which, because of all the dreadful things that have happened to Jack and me since that balmy summer night, have such tremendous significance.

Valerie said, 'Haven't you got a costume?' I couldn't very well say Stephen had thrown mine away, let alone try to explain why I decided to swim nude.

I just made a vague nod of the head and stepped back into the costume. Actually it was hers.

So the first time I met her husband, I also took his wife's bathing costume.

She described Ivanov (who had indeed, she said, been among her boy friends) as 'a wonderful huggy bear' of a man. Profumo had always worried about being unfaithful to his wife; she (Christine) and he had gone for long drives to avoid company. Once they went to see a George Ward, who had at that time been Secretary of State for Air, and she had flirted with him to make Profumo jealous. (The next day Lord Ward, as George Ward had now become, said he didn't remember any of this, and anyhow there would have been nothing wrong.)

For the first time, also, the place and function of Christine Keeler in the structure of the conservative emotional economy began to emerge. The very first night she met Profumo they went to Cliveden, and the men dressed her up in a suit of armour. Again, Stephen Ward

had an extraordinary sense of humour and loved creating a sensation. For instance, one of his little jokes was to put a dog collar round my neck and take me along the street on a lead.

Ivanov was often with us and we would go into a pub and talk as if there was nothing unusual.

I would be sitting beside Stephen with the collar round my neck, and we would pretend not to notice the reactions of the other customers.

So it was not simply her good looks which had carried her upwards. *Cherchez* not only *la femme*, but which *femme*.

Harold Wilson went to Moscow to pursue his international contacts as planned, but everyone else in British politics ran round in small circles shouting. Parliament was in recess, and the House of Commons could not debate Profumo's resignation until the following Monday; that gave a full week for the pot to boil, the plots to ripen, the points to be plugged. A public opinion poll was taken before the resignation was published; even then, Labour had the biggest lead in years. Lord Arran, a genial conservative Press columnist, subjective and extrovert to the point of eccentricity, said in his column that Ivanov had approached him through Lord Astor and Stephen Ward suggesting that the British Government should call a summit meeting during the Cuba Crisis. He had forwarded the matter to the Foreign Secretary, who had not pursued it. (Ivanov's judgement appears in this to have been on a level with that of the Nazi leader Rudolf Hess who flew to Scotland in 1940, thinking that if only he could have a word with the Duke of Hamilton he could stop the war.)

The Stock Exchange fell more sharply than at any time since Cuba. What is bad for conservatism, said the pundits, is bad for the British economy. More sophisticated pundits remarked that stock jobbers (the people who have stock available for sale) will often drop their prices as far as they can at a slight excuse in order to panic the more powerful brokers (who have money

31

with which to buy stock) into advising their clients to sell, so that they can then get a lot more stock on their books before the price goes up again the next day.

A Canadian called Robin Drury, whom Christine Keeler had appointed as her 'manager' a month before, and who had led her in and out of the Old Bailey by the hand, was dismissed by her, and announced a few days later that he would sue her for wrongful dismissal.

It was made known that the Lord Chancellor, Lord Dilhorne, had been asked by the Prime Minister to look into the whole matter. The Lord Chancellor is a member of the Cabinet, but the feeling that it would have been better to call someone in from outside was mitigated by the fact that he had been appointed just twenty-four hours before Profumo resigned.

But it was not understood why the existence of the inquiry was only announced five days after the resignation. Several ministers who were abroad were called home and the Cabinet began to be in very frequent session. The Prime Minister had returned from Scotland, looking like death.

On the Tuesday *The Times* came out with another ardent editorial which contradicted the Labour line; it was headed: 'It *is* a moral issue.' Britain had gone sloppy, never had it so good; material well-being, high hopes deluded; insidious, imperceptible, inexorable, and even, to end up with, blood, sweat, toil, and tears. The *Daily Sketch* applauded. *The Times* later ran many columns of letters, for the most part saying Amen.

It began to be mentioned that the night before Profumo had made his first statement back in March he had been hauled from his bed by the law officers of the Crown and interviewed half through the night, so that the statement had been in some sort a collective one.

By the Thursday, there was talk of Cabinet resignations; in other words, of a move within the Cabinet to get rid of Macmillan. The names of Enoch Powell (Minister of Health), Henry Brooke (Home Secretary), Sir Edward Boyle (Education), and Sir Keith Joseph (Housing) were mentioned. Lord Home, the Foreign Secretary, denied that he was thinking about it. For a couple of days the Press followed the state of Powell's conscience as it had followed the health of the dying Pope the week before. Articles were written about how sensitive he was, and what high moral standards he had. He was photographed going in to places and out of places looking very unbending. It was remembered that he was a good Churchman, and that some years before he had resigned from a junior post at the Treasury in protest against Macmillan's inflationary spending. Nigel Birch had resigned at the same time, but he had remained in haughty and pointed enmity with the Prime Minister ever since.

The other three ministers soon said they would back Macmillan in the coming debate, but it was not till the weekend that Powell, suddenly smiling again, said that he would too. It was hinted in the Tory Press that it had all been an invention of the wicked Nigel Birch.

The left-wing Bishop of Southwark, Dr Mervyn Stockwood, falling short of his usual originality of language, said that there was a smell of corruption in high places. Clichés came out from under stones: fathers, return to the values of our; stables, cleanse the national; Denmark, something rotten in the state of; thunderer (*The Times*). The *British Weekly* (Church of Scotland), firmly coupling might with right, complained that people abroad were getting the impression that Britain was 'finished not only as a military power, but as a moral power'.

Stephen Ward was refused bail.

The *Daily Sketch* ran a front-page photograph of Ivanov kissing the wife of his opposite number, the American assistant naval attaché in London. But Commander Murphy, for such was the American attaché's name, said so he had – at an 'Elizabethan' mead-party with two-handled cups. He had been there. He had not actually kissed Mrs Ivanova, because that sort of thing did not appeal to him. Besides, one of their handles was broken. So there was nothing in that.

Selwyn Lloyd, whom Macmillan had sacked from the Treasury the year before in one of the most offhandedly ruthless operations of political surgery since the Prime Ministers became more powerful than the Kings, blamed the falling away from standards at a political dinner. The *Daily Telegraph* wrote: 'At present the Conservative Party is a shambles.' And every day the police went on questioning and questioning girls. At the time it seemed they were going to clean up an organization; actually they were out to get Stephen Ward.

Lord Hailsham, the great panjandrum and all-rounder of Church and State, Lord President of the Council, Leader of the House of Lords, Minister for Science, Minister for Sport, Minister for the economically depressed area of the North East, Minister negotiating the Test Ban Treaty, Churchman, and lawyer, went on B.B.C. television and was magnificently cross. 'It is intolerable,' he said, 'that a man in this position should have behaved in this way.

'It is tragic that he should not have been found out and thereafter that he should have lied and lied and lied – lied to his friends, lied to his family, lied to his colleagues, lied to his solicitor, lied to the House of Commons.

'I cannot imagine a greater blow to public morality or integrity than that. . . .

'It is silly to talk about not being interested in Mr Profumo's morals. Mr Profumo's morals are a great public issue. . . .

'It is silly to make a party issue of this. A scandal can arise in one party or it can arise in another. . . .

'A great party is not to be brought down because of a squalid affair between a woman of easy virtue and a proved liar. . . .

'*The Times* is an anti-Conservative paper led by an anti-Conservative Editor. I am content to appeal to the country and to appeal to morality and common sense. . . .

'Of course, we have all been kicked in the stomach. . . .

'This is a national moral issue and scandals could occur from time to time in any party. And it is for that party, whichever it is, to clean up its own mess and not for people to pretend that the principles or policies of the party, or its ultimate patriotism, or the integrity of its leaders, are involved in the unfortunate shortcomings of its individuals.

'Who said *Lady Chatterley's Lover* was something like holy communion? Not a conservative minister, but a Christian bishop.'

The Independent Television companies protested hotly that this was scooped by the B.B.C.: political statements are supposed to be made on both channels.

Lord Balfour of Inchrye, the husband of Mr Profumo's

34

sister, wrote to *The Times*: 'Lord Hailsham had no mercy. "Why should he?" can well be asked. Yet surely such a proud and powerful Christian as Lord Hailsham could have shown some element of Christian charity in his denunciation of a man with a shattered life.'

The debate in Parliament the following Monday began to loom more and more threatening to the Government. There was a terrible intensity of feeling in some of the things said by Tory M.P.s. A back-bencher called Dr Donald Johnson said: 'I hold a marginal seat which I cannot possibly fight at the general election so long as Mr Macmillan is Prime Minister.

'It was the element of exhibitionism in this episode that has unfortunately brought both Prime Minister and party into widespread ridicule which it is impossible for any person of professional standing to answer on a public platform.

'In regard to the party Whip summoning me to Monday's debates, obedience to this depends on a moral authority which no longer exists as regards this particular Whip.'

There then came an episode which looked like being the most damaging yet. A man called Michael Eddowes, sixty years old, a writer, a former solicitor, and a member of a dining circle called the Thursday Club to which the Duke of Edinburgh also belonged, published a letter he had sent to the Prime Minister alleging that he had written to inform the Security Service back in March that Christine Keeler had told him Ivanov had asked her to find out from Profumo the date on which nuclear warheads were to be delivered to West Germany. Since then he had repeatedly inquired what was being done, but had been brushed off at various levels. Christine Keeler promptly denied it, but later admitted that someone else, not Ivanov, had asked her to do this. She never had, though.

The night Eddowes told his story, the Home Secretary was summoned back from Guernsey: he travelled in a warship.

During a by-election campaign the Tory candidate was driven off his platform by shouts of 'Vote for Christine'.

Time magazine reported that Mandy Rice-Davies recalled a dinner party at which 'a naked man wearing a mask waited at table like a slave. He had to have a mask because he was so well known'.

Christine Keeler formed a hundred-pound company, with Paula Hamilton-Marshall as co-director, so as to pay less tax on her income.

The general sensation of everything coming down around the establishment's ears was heightened by a pessimistic leader in the *New York Times*.

A political crisis even more profound than the storm over Suez which blew Anthony Eden out of office and brought Prime Minister Macmillan to power is now shaking Great Britain to its foundations. The Suez crisis forced a change in Conservative Prime Ministers but left the Conservative Government intact. The present crisis threatens to end the twelve-year rule of the Conservative party and bring to power another Labour Government – with far-reaching impact on Britain, Europe, the North Atlantic alliance, and the Atlantic community.

The *Washington Post* said that 'a picture of wide-spread decadence beneath the glitter of a large segment of stiff-lipped society is emerging'.

President Kennedy was due to spare Macmillan an hour or two the next week after he had done his real business in Germany. Perhaps he no longer should.

The possibility of the conservatives saving the ship by dropping the pilot was reduced when a poll was published which suggested that eighty-five per cent of conservative supporters thought Macmillan should continue as Prime Minister.

By the weekend, all normal activity seemed to have ceased in Britain. The *Economist* carried the title 'The Prime Minister's Crisis' with a picture of Christine; no other explanation. She was his crisis. He was ours. A letter appeared in a paper saying it seemed as though the entire national life of Britain had 'passed through the loins' of a girl of twenty-one. She was offered £5,000 a week for twelve weeks to commère a floor-show called Turkish Delight. Her solicitor, W. F. Lyons, said she would certainly not do it, and went on: 'The criticisms which have been levelled against her and her attempts to provide for her predictably difficult future show no appreciation of the reality of her situation. Those who speak of her without charity seem to take no account of her youth nor of the fact that since the age of fifteen her manifest immaturity has been constantly exploited by a so-called adult society.' The voice of sense and humanity sounded strange at that moment.

Away in Hollywood a stripper assumed the name of Pristine Keeler. The New York *Daily News* headlined 'Macmillan's sexmergency' and wrote the next day: 'Four in Mac's Cabinet weigh resignations as sex-pot boils.'

The second instalment of Christine Keeler's confessions showed a heightening in the style, but only one new titbit. Ayub Khan, the President of Pakistan ('like Ivanov, he was a real man; husky, suave, and incredibly virile for his age'), had once, she said, ducked her in the swimming pool at Cliveden. The stylistic change suggested a decision at the *News of the World* to build her up as a popular heroine, a girl just like any other except that things kept happening to her, a little wild, but typical of a new and healthier morality. There was no more talk of armour or dog-collars. 'There was the City talking about falling share values, and that place Wall Street was in a panic too. And there was little me, alone in my flat. . . .' The climax deserves quotation since it is an extreme but perfect vulgarization of the fulfilment-cult started in this country by Galsworthy and followed up by Lawrence. (Only five years ago, the *News of the World* was still faithful to John Knox.)

Here was my perfect specimen of a man. And he wanted me. He couldn't have stopped now anyway. We crashed across the room. A little table went flying. He pinioned me in a corner by the door. I relaxed. Because he was just kissing me with all the power of a man in a frenzy of passion.

I made one last attempt to get away. But he caught hold of me. Our very impetus carried us through the door, and we half-fell into my bedroom.

There was my little bed, with its blue coverlet, and the little pink dressing-table.

From that second I too threw all reserve to the winds. But I was still aware of what this meant to him. I was afraid he would hate me afterwards, because I knew that he was abandoning all his principles.

But he was like a god. . . . Clumsy perhaps, but only because he wanted me. He said so.

But later came the grim shadows, while he was lying beside me. I could sense his sadness; the deep black gloom that I am told all

37

Russians feel after they have done something they feel they shouldn't have done. He was sad, very sad. . . .

But we had been together, Russian man and English girl. What thoughts does a girl have on such occasions? The joy of fulfilment? The triumph of conquest? I do not pretend to remember.

But espionage? No such thought.

What had happened between us was something as old as time – something as vivid in Russian as in English or any other language on earth.

I never dreamed I might be the girl who rocked the Government. I know nothing of high affairs, or wanted to. All I know is that when I allowed Eugène to love me I was young and free.

In the world of high affairs, the seers got down to successors. The name of Reginald Maudling, the Chancellor of the Exchequer, was the first out of the hat. He was a grammar-school boy, the only one to have made good in this Government. . . .

At a meeting of Conservative Party workers, Lord Poole referred to more rumours. Somebody said: 'There is now a rumour floating around the country that a member of the Royal Family is involved with this lady. You see how important it is that the true facts should be put to the nation.'

Lord Poole replied: 'In these affairs, which are moving quite rapidly, it is not possible for me to say today what I will or will not advise the Prime Minister to do on Monday.

'The rumours that are going around are very serious indeed. I can only tell you that, having listened to what you have all said today, I will give him the best advice I can at the time.'

Another party worker said: 'It would be wrong for me to stand here and say there are no other rumours about members of the Government. It seems to me we are in a very weak position until these rumours are also cleared up. Don't let us close the Profumo chapter and open the book with another. Will you please say, sir, that is the end of it?'

Lord Poole said: 'There are rumours at the moment about everybody. It would be hardly possible to describe the horror. . . .'

He broke off at this point and paused for a few seconds before saying: 'Are we really to pursue each rumour? Is every man in public life to be subjected to a sort of M.I.5 screening before he is allowed to become a Junior Minister, in the same way as

McCarthy said should be done with the Communists in the United States? I don't think it is possible.'

Fantastic and unsupported rumours at this time alleged that Stephen Ward ran a real brothel and that his portrait drawings were done while clients were writing out the cheque, just so there should be something to show for the payment.

They also said that half a dozen other ministers had been to Christine and Mandy; that the man in the mask was a minister; that a minister had been photographed with Christine Keeler wearing only a masonic apron (Lord Hailsham later said it wasn't him).

Lord Poole said the Prime Minister was a Man of Truth, and the reassured Powell said that he was a Man of Conscience. This curious trick of Tory diction (Eden had gone on television the night he attacked Egypt and said that he was a Man of Peace) did nothing to reduce suspicion and disquiet.

The Chairman of the Church Information Committee wrote to the *Church Times* saying that it was all the fault of the Cambridge Theologians, and the Soviet News Agency, *Tass*, complained of the 'clumsy attempt by some British scribblers, in one way or another, to attach Ivanov to the Profumo case. Some circles in Britain do not hesitate to use any methods in the election struggle, without thinking of the danger to Anglo-Soviet relations'.

But the general claustrophobia reached its deepest when it was reported that Mandy Rice-Davies had once again been arrested; once again at London Airport; once again on her way to Majorca. This was where we came in.

CHAPTER 4

THE House of Commons began its great debate on Monday, 17 June, under multiple difficulties. To begin with, the Government had issued a three-line whip; this is a device to deprive members of the free judgement for the exercise of which they have been elected. It means: on such and such a day you shall be there and shall vote the way your party leadership tells you to. In his already famous telecast, Lord Hailsham had said that it summoned you to attend, but did not tell you which way to vote. It is indeed true that that is all that is written on the sheet of paper members receive, but it is by no means all that is understood. For this judgement, as we shall see, Lord Hailsham was soundly belaboured in the debate.

Although this might have been a debate which would lead members to decide whether or not they wanted a new Prime Minister, it was widely reported in the Press that all that had been settled in advance. Those who counted, and those particularly who counted with the '1922 Committee', as Conservative backbenchers are called, had agreed to produce a majority for Macmillan in return for his undertaking to resign a month or two later.

To go on with, the House of Commons was not debating a motion about the Profumo Affair at all; it was debating whether to adjourn. At half past three the Government Chief Whip, Martin Redmayne, rose and proposed that it should. Until ten in the evening it debated the Profumo Affair, and then voted on and passed Redmayne's motion. It did not, however, adjourn even then. This procedure is often adopted, and is traditional.

But by general assent, the debate was held to be about Profumo's resignation, and it was also generally understood that the aspect to be especially debated was whether there had been, or had been likely to be, a breach of security because of his link with Commander Ivanov. It was also generally accepted that this had been proposed by the Opposition, and agreed to by the

Government. This too is the time-honoured procedure; the House of Commons likes above all to avoid pinning itself down by admitting it is debating what it is debating.

A third disadvantage, and one which was taken more seriously at the time than the two former, was that Dr Stephen Ward was awaiting trial in prison. The House of Commons can say anything about anybody without fear of libel; it can say he is, for instance, a procurer, pimp, ponce, spy, murderer, or pirate, as long as he has not been accused before the courts of being such a thing. As soon as he has been accused, they can no longer say anything about him for fear of damaging his chances of being acquitted by the court of being a procurer, pimp, ponce, spy, etc. Cynics wondered whether Dr Ward had been arrested earlier than might otherwise have been the case (his trial did not begin for five weeks) in order to reduce the verve of the Labour onslaught in Parliament. They were probably wrong; the degree of control exerted by the Government over anything in the preceding weeks, let alone over things they were not supposed to have any control of, had been slight.

In spite of these quaint handicaps – a traditionalist would say because of them, but that would be hard to establish – the debate was a remarkably valid one. There was real distress in the country; worry and a kind of useless ardency of feeling. There had been repeated cries for 'leadership', and some *je m'en foutisme* of the sort which has not at any time in the twentieth century led to constitutional or political improvements in other European countries. There was a real public will to know what had happened, to know who was honest and who was not, who was idle and who diligent, and what might be thought about it all by those who knew more than Everyman. Answers were in very large measure provided by the debate. The House of Commons had no doubt had 'finer hours' when it expressed unanimous feeling in the country; there had no doubt been calmer and clearer debates during the measured and prepared passage of legislation; single speakers had no doubt shown greater wisdom and higher oratory when vaster topics were discussed; but seldom had it showed up so well as a place where confusion and dismay could be sorted out for the public good.

Harold Wilson opened for the Opposition. He outlined exactly what was to be talked about, and that was in fact what was talked about.

'This is a debate without precedent in the annals of this House. It arises from disclosures which have shocked the moral conscience of the nation. There is the clear evidence of a sordid underworld network, the extent of which cannot yet be measured and which we cannot debate today because of proceedings elsewhere.' [This was a reference to the pending trial of Stephen Ward.] 'I believe that the feelings that have been aroused throughout the nation are similarly echoed in this House and that there are many Hon. and Right Hon. Gentlemen opposite who are made as sick at heart by what has been disclosed as those on this side of the House. There is the personal and family tragedy of a man lately our colleague here. However much we condemn him – and we must condemn him – that is not the issue today.

'What concerns us directly is that the former Secretary of State for War, faced with rumours and innuendo that could not be ignored, chose deliberately to lie to this House, and in circumstances in which this House allows freedom of personal statement without question or debate on the premise that what is said is said in good faith.

'What does concern us, too, is the question whether any other Minister in any sense connived at this action through foreknowledge or, being in a position to ascertain the truth, failed to take the steps that were necessary to fulfil the duty that he owed to the House.

'What concerns us, also, is whether a man in a position of high trust, privy to the most secret information available to a Government, through a continuing association with this squalid network, imperilled our national security or created conditions in which a continuing risk to our security was allowed to remain.

'We are not here as a court of morals, though the nation as a whole cannot escape the responsibility so to act. But questions affecting national security, questions affecting the duty of Ministers to this House, must be pressed and probed today, and this debate, in one form or another, must continue until the truth is known so far as it can ever be known.'

Stephen Ward had been to see George Wigg, who had prepared

a memorandum. He, Harold Wilson, had sent this memorandum to the Prime Minister at the end of March. Going back through his own files, Harold Wilson found that Stephen Ward had also written to *him*, during the Cuba crisis, and used the word 'intermediary' about himself; he had forwarded Ivanov's approach to the Government. Harold Wilson therefore described him as a 'self-confessed Soviet intermediary'. He described George Wigg's memorandum as 'a nauseating document, taking the lid off a corner of the London underworld of vice, dope, marijuana, blackmail and counter-blackmail, violence, petty crime, together with references to Mr Profumo and the Soviet attaché. Quite frankly, I felt when I read it that if it were published as a fiction paperback in America Hon. Members would have thrown it away not only for what it contained, but as being over-drawn and beyond belief even as credible fiction.'

He had not made any of this public, 'and the implication, of course, was that the Prime Minister would handle his side of the matter with a corresponding sense of responsibility'. The Prime Minister's reply to Wilson's first letter referred to 'a' Stephen Ward, and was this not 'symptomatic of the indolent nonchalence' of his attitude throughout? He tried again, and on 14 May the Prime Minister had written to him: 'There seems to be nothing in the papers you sent which requires me to take any action.' Wilson went on: 'Nine days later, on 23 May, I received a further letter from Ward, who wrote also to the Home Secretary complaining of police inquiries directed towards his patients and saying that, because of these inquiries, he now felt it no longer necessary to conceal the fact that Mr Profumo had lied to the House. I immediately sent this letter, also, to the Prime Minister.'

He drew a contrast between the procrastination about Profumo and the brutal promptitude with which John Belcher, Parliamentary Secretary to the Board of Trade, had been investigated and broken under the Attlee Government fifteen years before. (Everybody old enough remembered that the accusations in this case had been bribery; bottles of whisky, and free sleeping-car tickets to Scotland. But in those days that had been a great scandal.)

The Prime Minister and the Leader of the Opposition had met

and discussed the Profumo matter, and as a result the Prime Minister had written again: 'I am sure in my own mind that the security aspect of the Ward case has been fully and efficiently watched, but I think it important that you should be in no doubt about it.' So Lord Dilhorne was set to work right through the Recess in order to satisfy the Leader of the Opposition who, inconveniently, was not so easy to satisfy as the Prime Minister, who was in charge of the nation's security. Why had not the Prime Minister announced the Lord Chancellor's inquiry? Because he was 'gambling on the issue's never seeing the light of day...'

'Let us be clear on this: whether there was a breach of security at any time, whether there was a leak of information, is something we shall never know.... There is no means now of finding out....

'The inquiries of both the security authorities and the Lord Chancellor were bound to be fruitless, because the Prime Minister does not know whether there was any leak at all. He cannot know. What we were concerned with was clear evidence that, leaks or no leaks, there was a standing condition of a security risk as long as the Secretary of State for War was part of this quadrilateral made up of Miss Keeler, Ward, the self-confessed Soviet intermediary, and Ivanov, the Soviet attaché.

'I did not myself think Ward to be a spy. He was too unstable for the Soviet authorities, who usually make use of better material: but he was undoubtedly a tool, an instrument, and his unique access to people in high places made him useful to them. But for a Secretary of State, a member of the Defence Committee of the Cabinet, with full access to all military secrets and to the military secrets of our allies, to be part of this dingy quadrilateral reveals a degree of security risk that no Prime Minister could tolerate for one moment after the facts were conveyed to him....

'Were they watched? He has to tell us this. The Prime Minister knows that it is a standing instruction in the security services that no Minister can be followed without the Prime Minister's express permission. Was it given in this case and, if so, will the Prime Minister tell us on what date permission was given to follow the Secretary of State for War?...

'When we say that there was a security risk we mean that

through a personal defect of character, or a perverted political or other loyalty, or through the possibility of intolerable pressure, or through cupidity or financial need, or through a personal or family relationship, an individual is more liable than his fellows to disclose information. That is what we mean by a security risk. To diagnose such cases is the whole basis of security work. Civil servants, War office clerks, engineers in Admiralty establishments, or workers in Ministry of Aviation contractors' works are frequently moved on the initiative of the security authorities if any security risk condition such as I have defined is found.

'Only two days ago we read that an Oxford undergraduate was barred from the University O.T.C. on a security initiative because his mother was born in Moscow.' [Laughter.]

Harold Wilson quoted from a recent White Paper in which a Conference of Privy Councillors had laid down the 'bible of security work'.

'"While confining themselves to the security aspect of these defects of character and conduct the Conference also record the view that in individual cases or in certain sections of the public service, a serious character defect may appropriately be the determining factor in a decision to dismiss a particular individual or to transfer him to other work."'

'Does this rule apply only to clerks, to civil servants, to workers in Government laboratories, or is there some reason why Secretaries of State are exempt from this condition?'

There came a warning about any further concealments.

'I say directly to the Prime Minister that if he purports today to give the House a full statement of everything that is known to him, and if, during the course of the next week or two, or the next month or two, there are more revelations, the House will hold him guilty, too, of misleading the House about the true facts in this situation. . . .

'I have already put to the Prime Minister, and will be putting to him, some questions to which I now know the answer on the basis of the Lord Chancellor's Report. I will not give the answers. I will leave it to the Prime Minister to give the answers, because it is right that he should decide how much of the Lord Chancellor's Report can be disclosed.'

45

The questions were four in number. (1) If the security aspects had been fully and efficiently watched, why had Ivanov not been declared *persona non grata* as a diplomat? (2) On what date was a full security watch put on Ward's flat? (3) When did the Prime Minister first hear the rumours? (4) Who told him? Had it not been a newspaper executive?

The Prime Minister later answered three of these questions, but never the first.

Harold Wilson now came to the logical crux of the matter.

'He cannot have it both ways, because either the Keeler-Profumo relationship was known and the security services were following it and there was no security risk, in which case the Prime Minister is very guilty for not having taken action over that period, or the security services knew nothing about it, in which case they could not have followed it and, therefore, the Prime Minister has no warrant whatsoever for saying that there was no breach of security, because he simply does not know. . . .

'I will hazard my own view of the answer. I believe that the first the security services knew or even guessed about this very big security risk was when a Sunday newspaper told them a few months ago. If this is true – the Prime Minister must be frank about this – this would imply that the £60 million spent on these services under the Right Hon. Gentleman's Premiership have been less productive in this vitally important case than the security services of the *News of the World*. He must tell us this. . . .

'So, though I personally acquit the Right Hon. Gentleman of foreknowledge or complicity in this matter – of course I do; of course we all do; I mean complicity in the misleading of the House – he cannot be acquitted of a grave dereliction of duty in failing to find out. The House was grossly misled and abused, not by his complicity, but by his inadequacy.'

Why had William Deedes, the minister in charge of Government propaganda, been present at the long night meeting where Profumo's lying statement had been approved by his colleagues, and why had not the Home Secretary? Macleod, the Leader of the House, interrupted to say that it was because Deedes had been the only Cabinet Minister present in the House earlier on when George Wigg had made his famous speech, and because the Home Secretary had 'left the House' before the end of the debate, and so presumably could not be found. Wilson said that if it had proved possible to get Profumo's solicitor out of bed and to the meeting, it should have been possible to find the Home Secretary and the head of the Security Service.

This was the gist of the Opposition's indictment on the political and factual level, and a formidable one too. But Harold Wilson did not leave the matter before essaying a general moral indictment, a field in which his touch is less sure.

'The reports day by day add to the odious record. Saturday's papers told of an opportunist night club proprietor who had offered Miss Christine Keeler – or should I refer to her as Miss Christine Keeler Ltd – a night club job at a salary of £5,000 a week, and I say to the Prime Minister that there is something utterly nauseating about a system of society which pays a harlot twenty-five times as much as it pays its Prime Minister, 250 times as much as it pays its Members of Parliament, and 500 times as much as it pays some of its ministers of religion.'

This one slight deviation into Tory values – for the proudest claim of socialism is that it will not measure people by money – opened him not only to the charge of not being able to spot blatant publicity stunting, but also to the following yodel of derision from Dame Rebecca West in the next ensuing *Sunday Telegraph*:

Nobody sensible would go to a night-club to see Members of Parliament coming down staircases dressed in sequins and tail-feathers unless there were at least 250 of them; you need a lot, as market-gardeners cunningly say when they are selling plants, to make a show. And if a minister of religion is not at least 500 times less useful to a night-club than Miss Keeler, then he ought to be.

The Prime Minister's answer to Harold Wilson's indictment relied not on hard rebuttal but aggrieved honesty.

'A great shock has been given to Parliament, and, indeed, to the whole country. On me, as head of the Administration, what has happened has inflicted a deep, bitter, and lasting wound. I do not remember in the whole of my life, or even in the political history of the past, a case of a Minister of the Crown who has told a deliberate lie to his wife, to his legal advisers,* to his ministerial

---

*Mr Profumo's solicitor was throughout this matter, and still is as this book goes to press, Mr Derek Clogg of Theodore Goddard and Co.

colleagues, not once but over and over again, who has then repeated this lie to the House of Commons as a personal statement which, as the Right Hon. Gentleman reminded us, implies that it is privileged, and has subsequently taken legal action and recovered damages on the basis of a falsehood. This is almost unbelievable, but it is true. . . .

'In a period of ministerial office which runs altogether to seventeen years, and more especially during the last six years as Prime Minister, I have had to face, like all ministers, grave and baffling difficulties. The House probably realizes, looking back on their character, that they sometimes involved great strain and pressure, but these burdens were all bearable because, whatever the different point of view between both sides of the House, whatever the degree of political argument and conflict, whatever the international dangers involved, these have been questions of policy. This is different. I find it difficult to tell the House what a blow it has been to me, for it seems to have undermined one of the very foundations upon which political life must be conducted.

'However, in recent days I have been trying to search my heart and conscience, and I have approached the matter in this way: there is the question of good faith, there is the question of justice, and there is the question of good judgement. I know that I have acted honorably; I believe that I have acted justly, and I hope that when it has heard my account the House will consider that I have acted with proper diligence and prudence.'

It was indeed the case that the first he had heard of Stephen Ward, or of Profumo's relationship with Christine Keeler and Commander Ivanov, had been when the 'general manager of a national newspaper' had told his principal private secretary about it on 1 February 1963. The Private Secretary taxed Profumo with the matter, and Profumo said what he later said to the House of Commons. He knew all the parties socially, but there had been no impropriety. (At this time, of course, Christine Keeler was not yet the 'vanishing witness'.) Profumo had broken off his relationship with Ward back in 1961, when he had been 'warned' by Sir Norman Brook, the Secretary of the Cabinet, that the Security Service had discovered Ward was a friend of Ivanov's.

Ivanov had first been introduced to Ward by Sir Colin Coote, who was among Ward's patients, at a lunch at the Garrick Club, held as a follow-up of a visit of naval attachés to the office of the *Daily Telegraph*, of which Coote was the editor. Ward was invited because he wanted to go to Moscow to draw people. (He later went to Tel Aviv to draw people at the Eichmann trial for the *Daily Telegraph*.)

On 8 June 1961 the Security Service had warned Ward 'of the need for caution' in dealing with Ivanov. Ward told the Security Service people that he knew Profumo and, the Head of the Security Service having informed the Secretary of the Cabinet of this, the latter warned Profumo 'of a possible security risk' on 9 August 1961. 'Neither the Security Service nor Sir Norman Brook had ever heard of Miss Keeler, or about the things that have now been revealed, or – I must be careful; they are *sub judice* – which seem to have been revealed in the Ward household.'

Profumo then broke off his friendship with Dr Ward. In his personal statement, he had said he had not seen Christine Keeler since December 1961; this had been an innocent mistake. He remembered having broken with her at the beginning of a parliamentary recess; actually it had been the summer recess, just after Brook's warning of 9 August.

'I must tell the House that Sir Norman Brook did not inform me either of the fact that he had received this information from the head of the security service, or that he had thought it his duty to speak a warning word about Mr Ward's friendship with Ivanov. He did not tell me. I have since consulted him and he is perfectly sure, in the minute he is perfectly certain, that his recollection is that he did not tell me.

'I do not complain of it. I merely state the fact that the minute that Sir Norman recorded makes no reference to his having informed me. He himself is in no doubt that he did not think it necessary to make any reference to me. I mention this at some length because one of the allegations which I have seen freely stated in the Press and elsewhere is that I knew of Mr Profumo's association with Mr Ward as long ago as August 1961, and I did nothing about it. This is the first charge of dilatoriness of duty that has been brought against me and it is completely untrue. . . .

'None of the authorities concerned knew at the date of the warning of Mr Profumo's acquaintance with Miss Keeler. If the private lives of Ministers and of senior officials are to be the subject of continual supervision day and night, then all I can say is that we shall have a society very different from this one and, I venture to suggest, more open to abuse and tyranny than would justify any possible gain to security in the ordinary sense.

'Moreover, the security services have not the resources to watch the houses of all citizens who number Russians among their acquaintances, and even though supervision of this kind were to be confined to those who are known to have personal acquaintanceships with members of the Russian and other Eastern European embassies in London the task would still be quite beyond the resources of the security services. In fact, it would be necessary to recruit an enormous army of invigilators, and that, I am persuaded, is not right, or the answer.'

At different times early in 1963, Profumo saw the Prime Minister's Private Secretary, the head of the Security Service, the Attorney-General, the Solicitor-General, and the Government Chief Whip. To all of them he 'confidently and emphatically denied the rumours in all and every important particular' and protested there had been no impropriety in his association with Miss Keeler. Profumo asked the Chief Whip whether he ought to resign, and was told he certainly should not, if there was no truth in the rumours. Why had not the Prime Minister spoken to Mr Profumo himself? 'First, I thought he would have spoken more freely to the Chief Whip and the Law Officers than to me, his political chief. Secondly, for me personally to carry out an examination of this kind, in the probing detail necessary, would have made it difficult, if not impossible, to have had – however innocent – social relations with him.'

He could have asked for Profumo's resignation; but he remembered what had happened in the Galbraith case.

'In that case, and again in the circumstances presented to me at this stage, I was anxious to avoid any injustice. I would ask Hon. Members: supposing I had required Mr Profumo's resignation and thereafter he had issued writs for libel – which, in fact, he did do – and had been successful – which, in fact, he was – that would have created the feeling that an innocent man had been unjustly treated by me. Quite apart from any personal considerations, the belief that any individuals innocent of any offence or misdemeanour could be victimized and their careers ended merely on the basis of rumour, which is subsequently shown by the judgement of the courts to be without foundation, would have a profoundly damaging effect upon the whole of political life.' The Prime Minister was mistaken here: Profumo's libel claims never came to judgement. The only one when money passed was settled out of court.

Since Profumo had denied the rumours, all the Government could do was to sit back and wait till someone libelled him. The *Westminster Confidential* story was no good; the circulation was too small and the 'general character' was wrong. The stories of Profumo's proffered resignation on 15 March were no good. Then came the speeches of Wigg, Crossman, and Barbara Castle on 21 March.

'Here then, at last, was an opportunity to nail the rumours, and nail them at once without the inevitable delay following the issue of a writ of libel. These allegations were made, I think, at a lateish hour, when I had gone home, and, I think, gone to bed. I was told of them over the telephone and readily agreed with a suggestion that Mr Profumo should now prepare a personal statement. It had to be done that night because next day was Friday and it had to be made as soon as possible, and, therefore, at eleven o'clock in the morning instead of 3.30 p.m. as is usual.

'Accordingly, Mr Profumo arranged for his solicitor to go to the House of Commons in order to make quite certain, as he was to make the statement, that it should be correct in every particular –' [laughter] '– as we then believed, as I think we all believed. That was the real belief. There were present my Right Hon. friend the Leader of the House (Macleod), the Minister without Portfolio (Deedes), the Chief Whip (Redmayne), the Attorney-General (Hobson), and the Solicitor-General (Rawlinson), Mr Profumo and his solicitor (Derek Clogg) – a man, by the way of great experience and, I understand, a member of a firm of high repute.

'Much has been made in the Press about this meeting and Hon. Members may ask why other Ministers should be concerned in a personal statement by one of their colleagues. The answer is because the Secretary of State was one of our colleagues and accusations had been made against him as a Minister as well as a man. It was essential that they should satisfy themselves that the statement should be unequivocal and should leave no room for criticism that any of the allegations had been smoothed over, or evaded. This they did. They were satisfied with his account, which was the same that he had given on all previous occasions.'

It had been said that they had a copy of the 'Darling' letter before them: that was not so. But:

'The knowledge that his letter might be published at any moment – that is the important point – made my colleagues feel confident that Mr Profumo could hardly dare to give a misleading account of the contents of this letter. Here, I should tell the House that the Ministers did not know the contents. They were aware, and I was made aware, that the letter began with the word "Darling". This was volunteered by Mr Profumo, who explained that in circles in which he and his wife moved it was a term of not great significance.' [Laughter.] 'I believe that that might be accepted – I do not live among young people fairly widely. ...

'I could not believe that a man would be so foolish, even if so wicked, not only to lie to colleagues in the House but to be prepared to issue a writ in respect of a libel which he must know to be true. So any doubts I may have had were removed. I thought it right to come to the House, and I do not reproach myself for that, to sit beside a colleague of my Administration while he made a personal statement refuting the damaging and scandalous remarks made about him.'

When the Lord Chancellor had been making his inquiries he learned that Christine Keeler had told the police on 26 January, while they were questioning her about the Edgecombe affray, that Stephen Ward had asked her to discover from Profumo the date on which certain atomic secrets were to be handed to West Germany by the Americans – this was at the time of the Cuba crisis – and that she did not put this question to Mr Profumo.

'I think it very unfortunate that this information was not given to me, but the head of the security service, in considering these reports, did not take that as of great importance.'

During the Cuba crisis, several people had forwarded messages from the Soviet Union, mostly suggesting that Britain should call a summit meeting. 'Ivanov, with the assistance of Mr Ward, was perhaps rather more persistent than most; but he was not the only one to try to bring this pressure to shake us and, by us, bring what pressure they could on the United States.' Another who had pressed in the same direction was Loginov, the Soviet Chargé d'Affaires in London. The motive had been to 'drive a wedge' between Britain and the United States: it had been 'part of the Soviet attempt to weaken our resolution'.

Harold Wilson's letters and George Wigg's memorandum had gone to the Security Service, but there were 'no new points' in them. At that time, Ward was still maintaining there had been no impropriety between Profumo and Christine Keeler.

The Prime Minister's speech so far had not greatly surprised anyone. If matters had not been as he described them, that is to say, that the Security Service had known a good deal of what was going on but had not informed him, he must have been as big a liar as Profumo, and this was not suspected. He turned now to events which were unknown to the public, and could hardly have been suspected by them. Stephen Ward asked to see the Prime Minister's Private Secretary on 7 May, and did so, the latter being accompanied by a Security Service man.

'It transpired that Mr Ward wished to complain about certain inquiries which the police were making at that time and which, as we now know, led eventually to his arrest. He was, of course, very properly told that this was nothing to do with me or, indeed, with any other member of the Government; that the police were charged with the duty and responsibility of investigating any alleged criminal offence and were not in any way in this country under political direction or control.

'During the course of his complaints, Mr Ward let drop the remark that Mr Profumo had not told the truth. This, of course, was the opposite from what he had been saying earlier in his conversation with Mr Wigg.

'As a result of these fresh allegations by Mr Ward, Mr Profumo was again closely questioned on several occasions and each time he firmly maintained the truth of his statements.'

It was after this that the Lord Chancellor was set to work.

Going back again in time, the Prime Minister said that back in March, just after the lying statement, Mrs Huish, Christine Keeler's mother (she had married again), had gone to her local police and said that a Mr Eddowes had suggested to her that

Christine should say Ivanov was her boyfriend and that she had got information from Profumo and given it to him as a joke. She would get five to ten thousand pounds from the papers for saying this ('an underestimate', said the Prime Minister) and would become a little heroine. Five days later the police went to Eddowes, and he told them Christine Keeler had told him she had been asked to find out about the warheads. Later he telephoned the police, and was told that 'the matter would be dealt with by the proper authorities'.

'This was at the beginning of April. From that date until 13 June, Friday of last week, Mr Eddowes took no further action although there had, of course, been sensational developments in the meantime. Whatever the reason for the timing may have been, Mr Eddowes wrote to me on 13 June and sent the letter to the Press. The House, I think, may draw its own conclusions of the way this story reads.' (For Mr Eddowes' account, see page 35.)

The Prime Minister ended his account with a brief description of the resignation of Profumo on 4 June, two weeks before the debate, and passed to his final plea.

'I would ask the House to consider what alternative I had except to believe what I was told by Mr Profumo. Here was a man who had been for a long time a Member of the House; who had a good war record; who had been appointed originally to a junior office in 1951 and had worked his way up the ladder. Why, then, should I disbelieve what he told me? Would I not have been guilty of great harshness if I had then demanded his resignation?

'The House will, therefore, realize what a terrible shock it was to me suddenly to be confronted with this dreadful admission, and all that it implied regarding his conduct towards us all. ...

'The Right Hon. Gentleman the Leader of the Opposition has suggested that it was only because of his insistence and the decision to ask the Lord Chancellor to make inquiries that Mr Profumo decided to confess his guilt. I fear I am not able to speculate on the reasons that impelled him to confess. It is true that it may have been because he was asked by the Lord Chancellor to come before him, but, after all, he had faced examinations by very able men – including the Law Officers – not just once but several times.

'There may have been other reasons. He may have felt the

54

pressure too heavy upon him. He may have been induced at last to open his heart to his wife. He may no longer have felt able to live with a lie. Or, to take a more cynical view, having heard that the activities of the police were leading to Mr Ward's arrest, he may have feared that out of this the truth would inevitably come. I have no grounds for deciding between these various speculations. ...

'Let me now summarize. I have told the House in great detail the whole story of this affair as far as I was concerned with it. I think that I have omitted nothing of importance – I hope not. I have certainly avoided nothing. I said at the beginning that it was my duty to act honourably, to act justly, and to act prudently. My colleagues have been deceived, and I have been deceived, grossly deceived – and the House has been deceived – but we have not been parties to deception, and I claim that upon a fair view of the facts as I have set them out I am entitled to the sympathetic understanding and confidence of the House and of the country.'

The rest of the debate added rather little to what had been said by the Party leaders. Harold Wilson had delivered a circumscribed attack where he thought it would damage the government, and where he thought the people wanted it delivered. On the narrow front of security – had the Prime Minister's indolence created a risk? – the attack was effective. The rest he had left aside.

The Prime Minister's reply commanded the respect which is due to frankness, but hardly the confidence which can only be earned by the addition of activity to integrity, and of judgement to faith.

Jo Grimond, the Leader of the Liberal Party, swimming as always in the oxbow lake while the stream flowed rapidly elsewhere, found little left to add to the attack.

Sir Lionel Heald, a former Attorney-General, rose to make some special points. He had discussed the matter fully with his successors, the present Law Officers, and with Derek Clogg, Profumo's solicitor. In effect, he was putting their side of the matter, especially about that all-night meeting.

When Profumo knew Christine Keeler, she 'was not in any way associated with West Indians, with hemp, or with anything of that kind'. When rumours first started, Profumo had asked the

55

Attorney-General (Sir Peter Rawlinson) what to do, and had been advised: 'The proper course for you to take in circumstances of this kind is to go to a solicitor of the highest experience. You have the right to absolute confidence with him. Go to him. Ask his advice and do what he tells you.' That is what Profumo did. He went to Derek Clogg of Theodore Goddard & Co., a very well-known firm of London solicitors.

'Hon. and learned Members of the other branch of our learned profession will know that if one wished to choose anyone to whom to tell, as one's solicitor, an untrue story, Mr Derek Clogg is about the last man in the world one would choose. He is a gentleman of great reputation. He has had great experience in cases dealing with libel, with divorce, and all those matters where human frailty and possible lying may come into account.

'Mr Clogg believed what he was told by his client. Mr Profumo told him – this I am authorized to tell the House – that he realized that the story was an improbable one, but he said to him: "I implore you to believe me because I know how difficult it is going to be to persuade you". He was cross-examined. The matter was gone into. On 3 February, Mr Clogg told the Attorney-General that he was satisfied that the story which he had been told was true.

'On 4 February, a remarkable event occurred. Mr Clogg and his counsel, a very well-known member of the Bar, Mr Mark Littman, visited the Attorney-General and informed him that an approach had been made by someone – I can say no more at the moment about that – to Messrs Theodore Goddard and Co. which appeared to indicate a demand for money. For obvious reasons, I cannot give particulars. (This episode is discussed on p. 110 below.) There was then a discussion and Mr Profumo stated that he desired to go, as he did go, with his solicitor and counsel to the Director of Public Prosecutions and ask him to take action. What stronger confirmation could Mr Clogg have of the truth of what he had been told?

'It is right and natural to ask – it is the question which I asked – why did not the Director of Public Prosecutions proceed? There will be Hon. and learned Members and Members on both sides of the House with knowledge of such matters who will know that there are circumstances in which it is difficult to take proceedings on a letter received from a solicitor unless certain evidence is available. I do not believe anyone will suggest that the Director of Public Prosecutions was engaged in any supposed conspiracy. In the event, proceedings were not taken.

'When Colonel Wigg brought up the rumours in the House on 21 March, the Ministers, particularly the Attorney-General, said to Mr Profumo, "The time has now come when you have got to deal with this situation. The only way you can do so satisfactorily is to make a statement in the House of Commons." He said that he would like to do this, so it was then said to him – I should myself regard this as a perfectly proper step – "In the circumstances, we had better ask Mr Clogg to come here and see that there is no question of your saying anything which you ought not to say."' [Hon. Members: 'Oh.'] 'Certainly. If Hon. Members will be patient, they will see what was meant by that. Mr Clogg came here. The Law Officers of the Crown drafted the statement, and they submitted it to Mr Clogg, asking him whether, in his view, it was right and proper that Mr Profumo should make it. We should not forget that he might have been incriminating himself. They did not know what Mr Clogg's attitude would be.' [Interruption.] 'Let us be patient for a moment. After all, these men are in the dock: they are entitled to be defended.

'The Solicitor-General has told me that he said to Mr Profumo, "You must realize that you are making a statement that there is no truth whatever in any of these allegations. Supposing that there is, for the rest of your life you will be submitting yourself to blackmail." Mr Profumo's answer was, "I quite realize that, but, as it is all true, I have nothing to fear", and, as we know, he made the statement.'

The speech of Sir Lionel Heald made it even clearer than the Prime Minister had made it that the four ministers had virtually submitted the matter to the judgement and experience of the solicitor Clogg.

Nigel Birch, whom it was believed Macmillan feared more than any other enemy on his own side, perhaps because he was the only man who was capable of appearing lackadaisically superior even to the Prime Minister, spoke with his accustomed disdain. He started out with the Press.

'In all these miseries, the fact that so many people have found some genuine happiness is something to which, in all charity, we have no right to object.

'I must say that I view the activities of the editor of *The Times* with some distaste.'

E. L. Mallalieu: 'First-class stuff.'

Mr Birch: 'He is a man about whom it could have been predicted from his early youth that he was bound to end up sooner or later on the staff of one of the Astor papers.'

(The other Astor paper is the *Observer*.)

Birch made a point which common sense could hardly contradict, though charity might have suggested other language:

'Here one had an active, busy man and a professional prostitute. On his own admission, Profumo had a number of meetings with her, and, if we are to judge by the published statements, she is not a woman who would be intellectually stimulating. Is it really credible that the association had no sexual content? There seems to me to be a certain basic improbability about the proposition that their relationship was purely platonic. What are whores about? Yet Profumo's word was accepted. It was accepted from a colleague. Would that word have been accepted if Profumo had not been a colleague or even if he had been a political opponent? Everyone must, I think, make his own judgement about that.'

He asked the Prime Minister to resign, quoting Browning, and wound up with a neat left and right at the inferiority of those among whom his convictions forced him to live.

'Ahead of us we have a division. We have the statement of my Right Hon. and noble friend Lord Hailsham, in a personal assurance on television, that a Whip is not a summons to vote but a summons to attend. I call the Whips to witness that I at any rate have attended.'

He was followed by a no less formidable parliamentarian, but one with a very different manner, Colonel George Wigg. These two men, Birch and Wigg, are standing examples of what happens to politicians who actually care. It is not enjoyable for them, but it can be very impressive for everyone else.

'I would not,' said George Wigg, 'pretend for one moment to be a Christian. If some of the ideas of Christianity which we have heard from Lord Hailsham are representative, then I confess that

I am a pagan, for the Christianity that I learned at my mother's knee taught me that it was something which had to do with redemption, and that there was not one Mary but two, and that Jesus loved them both. To use this occasion or any other when the Tory party is in a jam to pour out moralizing phrases, humbug, and cant from their mouths, is something that I can't take. ... Let me say frankly that if the moment ever comes when I see Lord Hailsham on one side of the road and John Profumo on the other, it is to John Profumo that I will go. ...

'Lord Hailsham is put on to broadcast. He is a great actor. He seethes with moral indignation. He is the great champion of truth. He claims this to be a non-party matter – the object being to try to make out that we on this side of the House have played party politics. Then suddenly he is in a jam. For a split second he finds himself in exactly the same jam as John Profumo found himself. Someone asked him, "What about the Three-line Whip?" He could have said, "You have caught me", but he did exactly the same as John Profumo did. He lied. There is not a Right Hon. or Hon. Gentleman on either side of the House who accepts Lord Hailsham's interpretation of what a Three-line Whip means. The Three-line Whip is the final appeal to loyalty on party lines, and Lord Hailsham knows it. Whether I am in order or not, I call Lord Hailsham a lying humbug.' [Hon. Members: 'Hear, hear.']...

The rest of his speech sprang mainly from his own relationship with the former Secretary of State for War, a relationship, as no one was likely to forget, between an extremely honest man and an extremely dishonest one.

'I make no claim for myself. The Prime Minister asked for sympathy. I ask for none, because there is one simple thing which Hon. Members know very well: that the Wigg family motto is, "Tomorrow is also a day" and that anything slung at me will in due course, God willing, be slung back again.'

He recalled the occasion when he, Richard Crossman, and Barbara Castle had first mentioned the story in the House of Commons. The Government had complained about the way his two colleagues had done this.

'Twice, it was said that they had raised this under the protection of privilege. Why were such words put in? Was it because the

Ministers had been engaged in an operation to find out the truth? Oh, no! They were engaged in shutting me up. That was the purpose of that personal statement by Profumo. That day I left here with black rage in my heart, because I knew what the facts were. I knew the truth, and I knew that, just as over the Kuwait operation, I had been trussed up and done again. . . .

'This is what I want to say again to the Prime Minister in relation to the late Secretary of State for War. Who chose him? Who put him into that job? He was put into that job by the Prime Minister to carry out a specific task, a task which Mr Birch or Mr Harrison, or other Hon. Members who know anything about defence and who care for the defence of this country, would not have carried out. What he had to do was to get 165,000 men by 1 January, and it did not matter twopence how he did it. What he did was to lower standards, and he lowered the rejection rate from seventy per cent to forty per cent. I do not say that he did not care anything about the Army, but it was not as much as I do, or he would not have done it.'

The speech of the stalwart Tory backbencher Sir Richard Glyn provided a neat circular discussion within the ranks of his party.

'I am sure that I speak for the majority of Hon. Members on this side of the House when I say that when we heard or read that statement we were absolutely, finally, and completely convinced –'

Viscount Lambton (Berwick-upon-Tweed): 'Not every Hon. Member was convinced. I myself expressed complete disbelief in the statement.'

Sir Richard Glyn: 'The noble Lord is perhaps not entirely typical of Hon. Members on this side of the House.'

The Labour intellectual Richard Crossman asked whether it was true that an unsuccessful effort had been made in January or February to get a D Notice issued about Ivanov. A D Notice is a request from the government to newspaper editors not to mention a certain fact or topic. His question was never answered.

He also asked why the Prime Minister had not asked the newspaper executive who came to see his secretary to tell him more about the rumours, and specifically what was in the 'Darling' letter. He revealed that this executive was a Mark Chapman Walker, whom he described as 'the man who used to run the Tory Party machine'. This question was not answered either.

Lord Lambton, like Nigel Birch a persistent critic of the Macmillan government and, like him, seeming to come from a higher world altogether, where people were at once more worldly and more honest, made another common-sense point.

'The whole case of the Government has been made on the fact that Mr Profumo's relationship with Miss Keeler was innocent, and it has been said that as he said it was innocent he deceived everyone. But his innocence was totally irrelevant. It would have been a much more dangerous thing had Mr Profumo not been going to bed with Miss Keeler, because then he would have been going to discuss things with her six times, for half an hour. My Right Hon. friend Mr Birch said that she was not a very literary woman. There have been from time to time great literary prostitutes, but I think Miss Keeler was a prostitute who was basically used for prostitution. What I never could understand was how these five members of the Government were apparently satisfied that because Mr Profumo had not been to bed with her that was the end of the whole affair.'

Ben Parkin, the member for the slum and rackets district of North Paddington, let a sudden breath of human reality in among the grinding of political pressures. His prose is seldom smooth, but he seldom speaks without making better-educated men sound hollow.

'Is no one in the House today going to say a word of compassion for the poor little slut who is at the centre of all this? I think of five men in a room in the middle of the night discussing how they can make it appear that the word "Darling" is not compromising in any way, when surely we need a little compassion to consider how these wretches get into the state that they do. It was not that she was short of someone to call her "Darling". It may be commonplace in certain stratas of society. There are many others like her. How much better it would have been if there had been some older man, a relative, who had been able to say, "Darling, come home; Darling, it is not worth it: Darling, what are you fighting against?"

'Of course there was a security risk in this and a political risk in relationships of this kind. There was the risk of the canker in our society. There are the wretched creatures, who, because of their personal circumstances, have a love-hate relationship with the father whom they have not got, or with any substitute father; they must both love and hate him and betray him. This is elementary. But where does a word of compassion come? It seems that some of the people who have been sounding off with their Pharisaical denunciations can never have had any problems in their own families. There would be far more compassion and understanding from the younger generation, from those who have to live in these circumstances, although they struggle against them and although they deplore and regret the breakdowns.

'This is what we must, somehow or other, get out of this debate. If people mean what they say when they write to me telling me not to talk "dirt", not to talk party politics, but to talk of what is best for the nation, if we are to get back to a real understanding of the principles of democracy, there must be some kind of purging and renewal of principle. What pleasure is it to me to see the Prime Minister a beaten and broken man today? I hope that the Tories will not just trundle him out, without thinking of what their own responsibilities are and how far they go.'

He was followed by another of the loyal Tory Sirs, Sir Cyril Black, who first demonstrated his close connexion with the world around by saying he had never heard any rumours, and then gave a new and original view of history.

'Security is not only a matter of the operations of M.I.5, of keeping Cabinet and defence secrets, or of retaining privately the knowledge which is possessed about H-bombs and new weapons. The security of the nation depends at least equally on the character of the people, and when the kind of scandal breaks which we have witnessed in recent days it is not helpful to the character of the people which it is our duty as leaders in the nation to try to maintain and uphold. If history teaches us anything, it is that great empires and great nations in the past have come to final overthrow and defeat much more because the life of the nation has been corrupted from within than as a result of the assaults of their enemies from without.'

Reginald Paget, who had earlier congratulated Profumo on his acquaintance with Christine Keeler, was now carried clean away by the strength of his sympathy.

'From Lord Hailsham we have had a virtuoso performance in the art of kicking a fallen friend in the guts.' [Interruption.] 'It is easy to compound the sins that we are inclined to by damning those we have no mind to. When self-indulgence has reduced a man to the shape of Lord Hailsham, sexual continence involves no more than a sense of the ridiculous.' [Interruption.] 'Yet this is the performance which made the Tory Party say, "Here is our missing leader." The moment he was cornered, by being asked about the Three-line Whip, what did he do? He told a lie.' [Interruption.]

E. L. Mallalieu: 'On a point of order. Is it in order for Hon. Members opposite to shout all the way through a speech of an Hon. Member on this side of the House?'

Deputy-Speaker (Sir Robert Grimston): 'It is not in order, but it often happens on both sides of the House. It is to be deprecated.'

(The things said about Lord Hailsham by George Wigg and Reginald Paget gave rise to a running guerilla between the two houses of Parliament that lasted for several days. Lord Hailsham retorted he really did believe that about Whips, complained of language which would not have been permitted if he had been a member of the House of Commons, and wrote privately to the Speaker, who refused, in spite of some pressure, to divulge the correspondence.)

Iain Macleod, winding up for the Government, added few new points. He threw yet more light on the relationship which existed between Profumo and his colleagues when he repeated that on 3 February Derek Clogg had gone to the Attorney-General and 'confirmed' that Profumo's denials were true. He repeated that the Security Service had known nothing of Profumo's relation with Christine Keeler until the end of January 1963. The last words said by the Government in its defence were as follows:

'But it cannot be denied, and we have not attempted to deny it, that there was a security risk. There are two phases to this. There was the possibility of a security risk from the beginning of February. Then the information which came to light was handed the same day to the Security Service. By that time, Commander Ivanov had left the United Kingdom. But, of course, a new and graver possibility of a security risk arose with Profumo's admission on resignation, for now it was clear that in a period in 1961, whether measured by weeks or months – and the evidence is so conflicting that it is almost impossible to untangle – a real security risk obtained.

'Nevertheless, because it was a security risk it does not mean that security information was obtained. But it remains true – and it was perfectly fair of the Right Hon. Gentlemen the Leader and the Deputy Leader of the Opposition to make this point – that security can never be absolute. The police deal mainly with crime, and the Security Service obviously with security. It may well be that there is an ill-defined area between the two and, of course, we should review the situation. What should we do?'

George Brown, the Deputy Leader of the Opposition, had earlier suggested that the matter should be pursued by a Select Committee of the House, which would have given room for full political pressures and manoeuvres to be brought to bear. It was the natural suggestion for an opposition. Macleod preferred to have an independent judicial inquiry, the findings of which might or might not be published, as the Government wished. It was an equally natural decision for a government, and that was what happened.

CHAPTER 5

*Hailsham
Maudling
Butler.*

THE voting at the end of the debate was ambiguous: the Government had a majority of sixty-nine. (To a country which had read about nothing but sex in the headlines for several weeks the figure itself seemed ominous, or a confirmation of continental maturity, according to preconceptions.) It should have been over ninety. Twenty-seven abstained. Those conservative members who wanted a new leader felt that it was 'just right' – that is, enough to make Macmillan think of going, but not enough to make any-one think of an election. Macmillan himself appeared downcast and shocked at the vote.

Things went from bad to worse for him in the next few days. Some of those who had voted with the government wrote in to the Whips to say that this was not to be construed as a vote for Macmillan to retain office. It was widely noticed that Reginald Maudling, the Chancellor of the Exchequer, was an extremely nice man. He had no enemies; or, put in more practical terms, he was everybody's second choice at that time.

The House of Commons on 20 June went quickly and without much heat through the requisite straightening of the record. It expressed its displeasure with Profumo for having lied to it, and Macleod, on behalf of the Government, spoke half-hearted words in retraction of the rude things which had been said about Messrs Wigg, Crossman, and Castle for bringing the matter up in the first place.

Profumo returned from the country and made a statement. 'He wishes to take this opportunity through the medium of the Press to repeat to a wider public his profound remorse. Beyond this, neither he nor his wife have anything further to say.'

The important matter was the leadership question. Factions arose and dissolved; alliances were sworn and unsworn; candidates were advanced to the toot of the trumpet and wheeled quickly away when some speck of clay or other was espied on their boots.

There was a good deal of discussion whether the Conservative Party even had the right procedure for choosing their leader, and whether it might not be better to have him directly and simply elected by the Members of Parliament, like the Labour Party. The conservative procedure, as far as anyone was able to make out, was formally the following: a recommendation would be made by the leadership (usually by the retiring Prime Minister, but in this case, everybody seemed to agree, Lord Poole) to a kind of electoral college consisting of the M.P.s, the peers, adopted parliamentary candidates, and the National Executive. This recommendation would be accepted, and the Queen would then know what to do, though she might listen to the advice of former party leaders as well. It was suggested that the electoral college should be given a free vote. This suggestion can hardly have been serious; the hereditary peers would have had an absolute majority in it.

Once again the most acute analysis of what actually happens appeared in *Private Eye*.

Although Britain is a 'democratic' country, many traditional procedures of government are not accompanied by the more vulgar 'manifestations' of democracy, such as 'voting', which flourish in other countries.

This is especially true of the traditional 'Conservative Party', an age-old body of men who govern England. These men in the light of hallowed custom conduct their affairs according to 'gentlemen's agreements' and such is their great mutual loyalty and respect that all decisions are assumed to be 'unanimous' and traditionally 'democratic'.

No more so than at 'The Taking of the Soundings' – an ancient ceremony which takes place on those rare occasions when it is felt that the Party should 'elect' a new leader. (It should be explained that there is usually no need for the ceremony to take place at all, the new leader appearing out of the traditional 'Mists of History' to be acclaimed by all and 'sundry'.)

Unlike most new-fangled organizations such as the College of Cardinals, the party does not 'vote' at such a time. What it *does* do is difficult to describe. Indeed, so ancient and time-honoured is the ceremony that almost all living Conservatives have forgotten what it is.

Suffice it to say that 'the soundings' are 'taken' from the Body Politic by the traditional 'Sounding Fathers' each representing one portion of the Body – these include time-honoured Lord Poole, 'elected' by the Prime Minister, and the traditional Lord Home.

66

Other venerable men represent 'the Voice of History' and are thought to speak for all dead Conservatives and those who are yet to come.

The 'soundings' are then brought together in the traditional 'Carlton Club' – a secret meeting-place of the Party, and once they have been 'weighed' (some, traditionally, are heavier than others) they are conveyed to the Great Oracle of Truth (or the Queen, as she is known).

By the mystical power invested in her she then speaks the name of the new leader, after passing over the rejected candidate, the traditional Mr Butler.

To the untrained observer this procedure may seem hazardous, or even 'undemocratic', but such is the mystical sense of unity and justice which prevails that the right decision is inevitably taken and the British People are thus given the leader of their choice in accordance with the highest principles of democratic liberty.

One of the concomitants of the weakening of parliament in the last few decades under the whip system had been the corresponding strengthening of the party caucuses, the Party Meeting of the Labour Party, and the 1922 Committee of the Conservative Party. Macmillan and his friends got away to a bad start to their campaign against change at the first meeting of the 1922 Committee after the Commons debate. One of the most loyal of the loyal Tory Sirs, Sir Derek Walker-Smith, hogged time at the meeting to tell Members that if Macmillan resigned, the Queen might not send for a conservative successor at all, she might send for Harold Wilson, or she might dissolve Parliment there and then, and Labour would obviously win. Sir Derek was right in theory, and something like this had happened in 1905. But though the monarch may in theory call anybody as Prime Minister, even a man who will advise her to dissolve Parliament, she is more likely to feel constrained by custom to call a man who can command a majority in the House of Commons, as indeed she did when in October, 1963, she called Lord Home. The decision whether or not a conservative successor would be called did not therefore belong so much to the Queen as to those who would or would not accord him a majority, namely those present in the room as Sir Derek spoke. But that was not the worst; no sooner had he finished saying this at their private meeting than he went

67

on television and told the nation the same thing. That week the Prime Minister's stock was very low, and, according to the usual leaked accounts, the next meeting of the 1922 committee saw much recrimination.

The enemies of Macmillan in the Party put it about that pressure was being put upon them to allow him to remain with the following five arguments: that the Profumo Affair was all a communist plot, that President Kennedy was coming in a couple of weeks and there had to be someone there to talk to him, that Macmillan was just going to get a Test Ban, that there was no obvious successor, and that he would go in his own time anyhow. Lord Poole said in public that if he were fired at that moment, the revulsion against such disloyalty would keep the Tories in the wilderness for ten years, and Macmillan himself spoke at a fête in his constituency in emotional terms.

'In forty years of political life I have tried to do my best both for my party and for my country. I will not make my whole life worthless or meaningless by being untrue to those convictions either through panic or obstinacy.

'I do not regret anything we have done, still less that we should put the clock back.

'I think you know me well enough to realize that any decisions which I have taken or have to take will be taken in the spirit in which I have tried to serve the country all these years.'

A few days later he declared in public that he hoped to lead the Party at the next election, 'all being well, and if I keep my strength and health'.

But his own rebels, particularly Lord Lambton, continued to threaten 'civil war'; the *Church Times* continued to call for a 'statesman who will recall all sections of society to the things that are of good report', and Harold Wilson, nicely calculating the place where a word from him would do most damage, said how shocked he was at the disloyalty of the Tories during this moment of crisis; the least they could do was to rally round the leader who had served them so well.

The Security Service naturally took a beating from the Press, and so did Lord Normanbrook, as Sir Norman Brook had become. This too rebounded on the Prime Minister, because once upon a time there had been a tradition that a minister did not blame his civil servants for anything which went wrong, but took the blame himself.

There came a by-election in Leeds, at the seat made vacant by the death of Hugh Gaitskell, the last leader of the Labour Party, some months before. Labour won, as it always does win this constituency, but by an increased majority. The lesson of the election was that the swing towards Labour was no more and no less than that which had shown up at the last two by-elections, before the Profumo Affair broke.

The political air thickened yet further when it was discovered that a man called Philby, who had been in the Foreign Office and had left to become a journalist, had been a double agent for years, and had skipped behind the Iron Curtain. He had also tipped off Donald Maclean that the security service were after him, back in 1951, just before he skipped. The Government contradicted itself a good deal, and the Labour Party started out in full cry, but suddenly dropped it after a private meeting between the Prime Minister and Harold Wilson. Evidently this one was serious enough to justify a truce in the party warfare.

The Security Service lost more standing still by conspicuously claiming a part in the discovery of a Swedish spy (working for the Russians) called Wennerstrom, and certainly gained none by inflating the defection, some time previously, of a Russian official called Dolnytsin to a point where the American C.I.A., rightly or wrongly, felt obliged to deflate it.

At one stage things within the Conservative Party got so bad that a few members got together and discussed the foundation of a 1963 Committee, which should be the organ of a new generation, in opposition to the 1922 Committee. The last action of the Government before the trial of Stephen Ward caused the whole matter to change direction was to bring on the by-election at Stratford-on-Avon, Profumo's constituency, in the middle of August. Some saw this as a defiant gesture of confidence, others as a way of increasing the conservative vote by choosing a time when the farmers and lodging-house keepers were at home, and the few industrial workers were on holiday.

The affair, naturally, continued. On the official level it was consigned to a judicial inquiry to be conducted by a judge, Lord Denning. The Opposition at first protested that this was too private, too likely to favour whitewash and cover-up, but in the end settled for it and reserved their fire for the time when the judge should report.

Lord Denning's terms of reference were:

'To examine, in the light of the circumstances leading to the resignation of the former Secretary of State for War, J. D. Profumo, the operation of the Security Service and the adequacy of their cooperation with the police in matters of security; to investigate any information or material which may come to his attention in this connexion, and to consider any evidence there may be for believing that national security has been, or may be, endangered; and to report thereon.'

The Prime Minister said in Parliament that these terms should be able to cover all the rumours that were 'affecting the honour and integrity of public life'. He would publish as much of the report as seemed right, 'on security and other grounds'. Opposition outburst: what other grounds? Confused reply.

When Lord Denning began work, he was reported as saying it would take him some time; there would be more than twenty people to see. Two months later the Prime Minister himself was Lord Denning's hundred and sixtieth, and last, witness.

On the Press level, interest shifted from Profumo to a slum landlord, dead for eight months, with the suitable name of Peter Rachman. He had been known not only to his tenants but to everyone interested in the problems of metropolitan housing and race relations for years, but now that it appeared he had kept Mandy Rice-Davies for a time, and, in addition, was dead so that libel didn't come into it, he became a national scandal. He had used retired boxers and Alsatian dogs to push his tenants around, and had even taken the roof off one of them. Perhaps he was not even dead. Parliament roared, the Press roared, and the bishops obediently switched their denunciations from sex to rent profiteering. In time the Prime Minister appointed another inquiry under another lawyer.

The *Daily Mirror* announced in colossal type that rumour connected Prince Philip with the Affair and in quite small type that the rumour was unfounded. Lord Francis-Williams in his *New Statesman* column called the *Mirror* 'as lethal in defence as in attack'. Many newspapers savaged each other; it seemed for a time as though dog had ceased to bite anyone but dog, while dog-collar snapped also at dog-collar.

The tangle of events related to Stephen Ward and his associates continued to grumble. Eddowes recorded his story (see p. 35) for a television company, but then asked for the tape to be withdrawn and dashed to New York with a private detective. He wrote in the *Journal-American* that he would publish there his findings about what the American Intelligence Services thought about it all; they had been 'central to the case' since the time of the Cuba crisis. He never did.

A hitherto unknown character called Lawrence Bell, a reporter on the *People*, was accused of indecency with Guardsmen, and his counsel said that he had been framed by the police in order to stop his mouth about the Profumo Affair. Lord Denning saw him. At his subsequent trial, Bell was acquitted on all counts.

The Pakistan High Commissioner sent the *News of the World* a statement saying that President Ayub Khan, though he had lunched at Cliveden, did not remember meeting Christine Keeler there.

In the Profumo debate in the House of Commons the Attorney General had said that the last time Mandy Rice-Davies was arrested on her way to Majorca the police had been able to detain her, as they had not been able to detain Christine Keeler when she vanished before the Edgecombe trial, because there was a charge against her; there was no power to detain witnesses in this country against their will. Three days later the Home Secretary said in Parliament that there was no charge against her, but that she had entered into recognizances to appear as a witness at the trial of Stephen Ward. She herself added the detail that the police had taken away her passport. At the Ward trial it turned out that there had been a question of charging her with improper possession of a television set. The episode remained obscure; whoever had been correctly informed, it was not Parliament.

The *News of the World* stated that the party where someone had waited at table wearing only a mask had been given by a girl called Mariella, the wife of a certain Hod Dibben. She said that they had eaten peacocks, but that the man in the mask was not a public figure, only titled. Her father, whom she had not seen since infancy, had been a Czech, and she was related to President Novotny of Czechoslovakia. Three years earlier she had been arrested in New York in connexion with a call-girl investigation, and a man arrested at the same time, a British television producer called Towers, was now in Prague.

Three coloured American airmen who had met Christine Keeler were recalled to the U.S. and investigated, but returned to duty shortly after. Christine Keeler and Mandy Rice-Davies had their American visas cancelled.

Christine Keeler did screen tests for her proposed movie and those in charge said that less gifted people had made a go of it.

A firm importing foreign papers and magazines into Britain calculated that they had already had to censor forty-two publications for fear of libel.

The third and last instalment of Christine Keeler's memoirs in the *News of the World* denied that she knew any other minister beyond the three already mentioned, and was mostly about her childhood.

My stepfather brought me up as he would have done a son. He was incredibly strict – and tough. If I carry myself well now it is because he made me sit up straight at meals.

Once I was bitten by my own little dog. My father said it had turned vicious and insisted it should be destroyed, and that I should take it to the vet to be put away.

I said I couldn't do it. But he replied that I would have to take it. He said that I would have to get used to hardships.

One of my childhood girl friends used to hit me; she was a couple of years older than I. I used to go in crying to my parents.

Father would say, 'You get out there and hit her back, otherwise I'll give you a good hiding.' I can remember my mother crying as I went out and did just that.

But in spite of all this, I loved that stepfather of mine very dearly.

Robin Drury had a tape recording, lasting ten hours, of Christine Keeler talking about herself. The *News of the World* said they had refused to buy it for £20,000. It was believed that it contained things which conflicted with the evidence on which Lucky Gordon had been jailed. The men Gordon had asked for as witnesses, Commacchio and Fenton, turned up and made statements. Both were coloured. Commacchio was sentenced to three months for living on immoral earnings: his wife's, the court was told. He had sat in a parked car while she hustled.

Gordon applied for leave to appeal, and the Court made an order for a 'thing' to be produced; this was the tape recording. The Act in question antedated magnetic tape. A few days later the appeal was allowed, and Gordon went free, from which event another chain of scandal started.

Meanwhile, the foreign Press had printed a very great deal. The *Ghana Times* had said that it was easier for Ghanaians to avoid this sort of nonsense because they had Nkrumah to emulate and look up to. The Indian Press personified as Keelers the industrial concerns which were alleged to be bribing ministers. The German papers were rather impressed; Strauss had not resigned immediately he was detected lying to the Bundestag; he had had to be forced out, and Adenauer had said he was sure of a great political future. Some Italian papers had the same feeling, and one even ran an imaginary story about a minister in Rome, of Sicilian origin, called Giovanni Profumi, who had the same adventures and never dreamed of resigning. A good many papers, especially in the Latin countries, were surprised and pleased to find that sex was not after all unknown in England.

There was naturally a field day for all the rumours which could not be printed in England for fear of libel. As is usually the case with such rumours, some subsequently turned out to be true and others did not. The biggest single collection was printed in *Candide* on 3 July.

The Toronto *Globe and Mail* said Profumo held up a dark mirror to all of us, and the Western World as a whole could not just forget about him. Anthony West, arriving in England from the United States, wrote in the *Spectator* that Harold Wilson, and especially Richard Crossman, reminded him of Senator Macarthy. The Spanish papers were glad to be able to photograph Christine Keeler and Mandy Rice-Davies on Spanish beaches: after all, they were very pretty, and if they were less than excellent citizens, that was somewhere else.

By a long way the outstanding analysis of all those which I have read in mountains of foreign Press comment was that of

Pierre Accoce in *Noir et Blanc* for 8 August. This brilliant and unruly article is reproduced as an appendix (p. 113).

On 22 July Stephen Ward's trial began, and so did an exhibition of his drawings. These were pretty and competent, in a rather Royal Academy manner, but external, almost alienated, work. The heads of young women and eminent men loomed from unreferred backgrounds, often with a whitish, deathlike bloom on them. The Holborn Borough Council tried to close the exhibition saying that the premises were not licensed as an art gallery, but did not succeed. The pictures sold for large sums of money, but the royal portraits were priced highest of all, and remained unsold for some days until a mysterious grey-haired man in a bowler hat turned up at opening time one morning, bought the lot for just over £5,000 cash, in £5 notes, and took them away wrapped in brown paper.

It was already well known to the entire literate population what the prosecution case would be at the trial, since it had been fully stated and fully reported at the committal hearing, only three weeks before. Ward had been charged with living on the immoral earnings of prostitutes on three counts; one referred to Christine Keeler, one to Mandy Rice-Davies, and one to a period of time during which a prostitute called Margaret Richardson, *nom de guerre* Ronna Ricardo, was alleged to have visited his flat. He was also charged on two counts with procuring girls under twenty-one to have illicit sexual intercourse, on two counts with procuring abortions, and on one count with conspiring to keep a brothel.

Christine Keeler had said that she was not a prostitute, but admitted having taken money from Profumo, a certain Jim Eylan, a businessman, and from other men. The money Profumo gave her had been intended as a gift for her mother. She had lived in Ward's flat, and had given him some of the money she earned. Mandy Rice-Davies said she had been kept by Peter Rachman for some time, had slept with Lord Astor and Douglas Fairbanks among others, had had her rent paid by the former, and had on occasion paid rent to Stephen Ward when she was living at his flat. (When she was faced with Lord Astor's denial the next day, she said in court: 'He would, wouldn't he?') Ronna Ricardo's evidence was confused: she had been once or twice or

74

three times to Ward's flat, had slept once, or more, with a man, had, or had not, received money for it, but had certainly never given any to Ward.

The procuring charges had puzzled many people. It seemed that Christine Keeler had helped Stephen Ward to make the acquaintance of girls he liked the look of, and that Stephen Ward had then slept with them. But it was Stephen Ward who was charged, not Christine Keeler.

Mandy Rice-Davies in the magistrate's court said that the possible charge against her which might, or might not, have justified the police in taking away her passport, had concerned the possession of a television set and had been 'cooked up, anyway', and the defence counsel suggested with some force to police witnesses that they had been holding it over her head until she testified against Ward. She asked the magistrate if she could have her passport back, and he said: 'Certainly. If you don't get it back, you can consult legal advisers.' A police officer gave evidence that he had interviewed '125–40 persons' in order to prepare the case against Ward, and one of them, Christine Keeler, twenty-four times.

At the end of that hearing, Ward was committed for trial on the poncing, procuring, and abortion charges; the magistrate declared that there was no *prima facie* case on the brothel-keeping charge. Between then and the trial, the prosecution decided not to proceed on the abortion charges. They could have been held over for a later trial if he should be acquitted on the others.

On 22 July, then, the euphonious but anachronistic machine of British justice rolled into action at the Old Bailey. It so happens that the courtroom in which the most important criminal trials in Britain are held will contain about the number of people who are usually likely to drop in to any old trial, just to see a court at work, and no more. The public gallery, from which the proceedings are audible, was occupied by those who had queued all night in the street. A downstairs gallery was occupied by the privileged of one sort or another. The Press, and others whose job it was to make up for the smallness of the court by telling the world what was happening, found many of the places supposedly reserved for them occupied by the relatives of policemen. It is in any case impossible to see or hear from most of the Press seats since the dock where the prisoner sits is directly in front of them, separating them from the judge and jury, and is surrounded by a wooden screen about the height of a man, which is in turn surmounted by another two or three feet of glass. Any Press man who threatens to be so disrespectful as to stand in a place where he can hear is instantly expelled by the police. The judge, prisoner, and counsel are thus protected from the tomatoes the Press is no doubt longing to throw at them, and the Press is equally protected from seeing or hearing the justice that is no doubt being done. The jury is hardly less at a disadvantage than the Press; the witnesses face the judge but half turn their backs on the jury.

The charges contained one fine example of how to put first things first: '. . . attempted to procure Miss X, a girl then under the age of twenty-one, to have unlawful sexual intercourse with a third person, against the peace of our sovereign lady the Queen, her crown, and dignity.' The public was thus left in no doubt from the beginning that Ward's real fault was not that he had done harm to any particular individual – this was so unimportant that a mere capital letter would serve – but that he had acted against the system of values summed up by 'her crown and dignity'.

The procuring charges were not pressed with much avidity by the prosecution, and Ward was in fact acquitted of them. Ward and Christine Keeler had picked up various girls, and Ward had later made love with them. According to Christine Keeler, he used to discuss them with her afterwards. But, unless the charges were to be brought against her and not against Ward at all, it would probably have been necessary for the prosecution to show that he later passed them on to other men, and this they did not seek to do.

The prosecution was conducted by Mervyn Griffith-Jones, Senior Treasury Counsel (that means, trusted barrister often used by the Government for prosecutions), the very man who in the other great sex case of the decade, the prosecution of Penguin Books for publishing *Lady Chatterley's Lover*, had seen his grinding, contemptuous, authoritarian philistinism roundly defeated by the urbane and reasonable tolerance of Gerald Gardiner. That trial had been a duel of big men. James Burge, who defended Stephen Ward, was no Gardiner. He had one or two happy moments – ('my learned friend could make a honeymoon sound obscene') but in general he was slower off the mark than his antagonist. Griffith-Jones's Old Testament manner and four-square good looks conceal a supple intelligence. One could sometimes hear the astonishment in his voice at not yet having been stopped by the judge or objected to by the defence, and one could always admire the courteous deference with which he gave way when he was. He once permitted a police witness to read out a long section of a contested police record of one of their interviews with Stephen Ward, which dealt with the insignificant client Jim Eylan, and stopped him when he came to a passage about the sufficiently punished in-grouper John Profumo – but not before the witness had read out the following words, alleged to have been addressed by the policeman to Ward: 'He' (Profumo) 'has given Christine Keeler money in your presence.' Those who were in court will not soon forget, either, the way he referred to that highly urban chick Mandy Rice-Davies as: 'This girl who has just come up from Worcestershire'. Where the apples ripen on Balsall Heath.

The poncing charges were of two kinds. There were those about Christine Keeler and Mandy Rice-Davies, who had been his friends, and where it was a question of showing whether or not he had crossed the rather hazy line between what is disreputable and promiscuous and what is just, but only just, criminal.

The other kind were sustained by Ronna Ricardo and a new witness called Vicky Barrett. Both these were professional prostitutes; Vicky Barrett was actually a street-walker. She had been produced by the prosecution at the last moment, because the police picked her up one night for hustling and found Stephen Ward's telephone number at the head of a list of six clients in her diary. She had not known he was being tried, since she didn't read the papers. She had gone two or three times a week to his flat for two and a half months, had done business with naked middle-aged men whom she found waiting there, sometimes using a cane or a horsewhip, and Stephen Ward had promised to bank the money for her, though she had never seen any of it. These two witnesses belonged to a different world altogether, the world of professional, 'sordid' prostitution. The evidence conflicted sharply with the picture of Ward's life and personality which came out at the trial.

77

He spoke well as a witness in his own defence. He had two distinct manners. Sometimes he would stand bolt upright, answering, Yes, sir, and No, sir, as if he was still in the Army, with a deep and pleasant and frank-seeming voice. This manner seemed to make a good impression on the judge and the lawyers. At other times he would stand aside from himself, and get interested in something which had been said. Then he would lean forward over the front of the witness box and begin to gesticulate, talking in longish sentences and making judgements of events and people, including himself, as though he were outside it all. This manner suggested a desire to have a civilized discussion in the light of modern psychological hypotheses: it made a bad impression and he was frequently shut up. The witness who tries to tell an English criminal court something in his own terms, unless indeed he is so uneducated as not to be able to understand the lawyers', gets short shrift.

Ronna Ricardo changed her story. When she was called at the Old Bailey, she said she had lied in the magistrate's court. She had only been to Ward's flat once, and that time had led to a non-mercenary foursome. The rest she had said because she was frightened of the police. She was frightened that they would send her young sister to a remand home, that they would separate her from her baby, and that they would nick her brother for poncing. The reaction of the court was all in due form and order. The prosecution made an attempt to prove that she had been put up to it by the *People* newspaper, who had indeed spirited her away for a few days between the committal hearing and the trial. The judge instructed the jury to ignore her whole testimony, simply to put her out of their minds either way. That was all he could do. This was the first time that it became obvious for all to see that someone, some group or pressure, was really out for blood, and let justice go hang.

Vicky Barrett was detected in one rather small and not crucial lie, and thus too doubts were sown. Her evidence was also contradicted by some witnesses incidental to it, particularly by a society portrait painter, who, she said, had been one of the clients Ward introduced her to for business. This he denied. This Vicky was a really downtrodden little creature. Ward admitted having used her: 'I drew her, I had intercourse with her, and I paid her' – one could hear the rhythm interrupted by the poly-syllable required in court – but she was not part of his main-stream, as Christine Keeler and Mandy Rice-Davies were. The jury acquitted him of the count concerning Ronna Ricardo and Vicky Barrett.

They found him guilty about Christine and Mandy. The form of the law was such that their finding involved a decision that these girls were indeed prostitutes, and that he had indeed taken money from them in return for goods or services which were necessary to them for the pursuit of their calling. To one observer it appeared that in human terms, in real life terms, in the terms which naturally become meaningless when what must be held meaningful are the dry texts but not the living intentions of Parliament, what had happened was this; he had not taken enough care to avoid taking their money. During the time in question his income from his osteopathic practice and his portrait drawings had been about £5,500 a year, but he had received a few tens of pounds from the girls. In return he had put them up, and fed them, and ticked them off for using the telephone so much and leaving the lights on. Christine Keeler gave evidence that though she had given some money to him, she had not nearly repaid what he lent her.

On the seventh day of the trial the judge began his summing up, but had not finished at the end of the working day. Such was its effect, however, that Stephen Ward committed suicide. The judge adjourned the court, and the accused went home. Ward sent for a *Daily Express* journalist and paced up and down smoking. He had called Christine Keeler and Mandy Rice-Davies his bush-babies. He was afraid. The judge was in a hang-ing mood. Later he took an overdose of barbiturates and when the court met the next morning the judge cancelled bail and ordered a watch to be kept on Ward to see that he didn't try on anything else. He continued to sum up while the prisoner lay in St Stephens Hospital in Chelsea with a tube stuck into his windpipe through a hole, having air pumped in and out of his lungs. The jury returned their verdict of guilty on two counts out of five. Ward's suicide notes were found. He was sorry to disappoint the vultures. Ronna Ricardo and Vicky Barrett should please go to Lord Denning and tell the truth. (Vicky

Barrett cried when she received this message and told the Press that she had not thought of its coming to this when she lied to the court.) Three days later Stephen Ward died.

Parliament recessed, and for once the old talking-shop was really missed. Where else, for instance, could the extraordinary matter of Gordon's successful appeal be discussed? How could it be that in England, the proud home of 'not only be done, but manifestly be seen to be done', a man sent to jail by a judge with stinging words of reprobation only a month or two before could be suddenly released on new evidence without that evidence being made public? How could it be that in England, the home of common-sense law, it could be claimed that the unpublished evidence was not really evidence, because the Appeal Court was not allowed to have the witnesses put on oath, and for that reason it could not be published? This was the worst sort of secrecy in the administration of justice; the new fact was fact enough to cause the man to be let out of jail, but not fact enough to be told to the people. This means that the people must have blind faith in their judges, which is against reason and justice.

But a few weeks later, Christine Keeler, on whose evidence Lucky Gordon had been condemned, was arrested, and charged with committing perjury at the trial, and whatever it was that could be done at so late a stage began once again to be seen to be done.

General worry about justice and its administration was greatly increased by two horrible-sounding cases. In one, two young policemen in Sheffield were accused of beating up suspects with whips and truncheons. Their defence was that they had been ordered to do so, and that their senior officers had been present. In the other (first reported, as usual, by *Private Eye*), a man died after the following sequence of events. He was knocked down by a car, taken to hospital, treated for slight injuries, and then handed over to the police because he had reefers on him. He was returned to the hospital a few hours later very seriously injured. He survived in a coma, for a week, with a police watch at his bedside, during which time his former wife reported him missing to the police and was repeatedly told they did not know of him. When this story broke, the police, after six months' delay, appointed one of those pointless inquiries conducted by themselves into their own affairs.

And all the time the fact that two prostitutes had changed their stories in the Ward trial remained unforgotten and unexplained. It was an ugly season, and marked the end of English claims to superiority in these matters.

At the end of September the Denning Report, which was to put an end to all speculation and tell everybody what was what, was published. It was a well-written document, clear and even racy in style, tolerant in judgement, and humane in feeling, but more inclined, as one would expect from a judge, to inquire whether a crime or crime-like action might have been committed rather than whether a right or wrong decision might have been made. Denning discussed the gaggle of rumours about ministers' sex-lives (the headless man, the man in the mask, and all the rest), in most cases tracing them back to some innocent origin.

He supported Stephen Ward's version at his trial against Christine Keeler's in her newspaper article by holding that she and Ivanov had never 'become lovers', as he put it. This opinion he held in spite of (or perhaps because of) the two bottles of whisky which she and Ivanov got through alone together one night (para. 246).

He went back to the origin of the whole scandal in Parliament, and asked whether Profumo or Ward had helped Christine Keeler to leave the country during the Edgecombe trial. He examined their bank accounts, and found no evidence they had. But Paul Mann, the young man who took Christine to Spain, refused to allow him to examine his accounts. The allegation thus remains incompletely refuted.

It was made public for the first time in the Denning Report that 'the head of the Security service' had, 'got the impression' that Mr Profumo had hoped he would 'get a D notice or something' issued to prevent Christine Keeler publishing her story. As Denning said, Profumo's hope was a vain one. A D notice is something issued by the Government to newspaper editors, telling them that in the Government's opinion it would be against the national interest to discuss such and such a topic or person or affair. Its legal status is quite obscure; it is just one of those British bits which seem to work as long as no one complains. Profumo seemed to have hoped that the Security Service might already have recruited Ivanov as a double agent, in which case they might easily have agreed to slap a D notice on the whole business. But they hadn't; and the chance of Fleet Street's not complaining at having a D notice slapped on a Minister's girlfriend must have appeared to the Security Service so slight as to endanger the whole system.

It also came out for the first time that Profumo's solicitors had gone to see Christine Keeler to see if she could be persuaded not to publish her story (para. 95 and 112). This firm, Theodore Goddard, of which Derek Clogg (see page 56 above) is a senior partner, went on 2 February to see Christine Keeler at, (according to Profumo), her request 'since she said she was in trouble' (para. 128) and had 'some discussion about the contract', under which she had already received £200, with £800 due if and when the newspaper (the *Sunday Pictorial*, at that stage) published. 'The impression they got,' continued Lord Denning, 'was that she wanted money' if she was to withdraw her story. They suggested the name of a solicitor she might instruct to handle the matter. She went in fact to another, and this solicitor telephoned to Theodore Goddard and 'after a little to and fro', as Lord Denning put it, 'said £3,000. Mr Profumo's solicitor said he would take instructions'. When the request was a very short time later increased to £5,000 Mr Profumo's solicitors regarded it as 'so serious' that Mr Clogg went with his client and Counsel to the Attorney General and said that an approach had been made that appeared to indicate a demand for money. Profumo said he was prepared to prosecute, but the Director of Public Prosecutions, consulted the next day, advised against it. Christine Keeler's solicitor also went so far with Stephen Ward's legal representatives that £50 changed hands. The money came from Lord Astor to Ward, though Lord Denning accepted a correspondence between the two men as evidence that Astor did not know what the money was for. The £50 was on account of a larger sum about the amount of which there was a misunderstanding, and the deal fell through.

On the official side, Christine Keeler's story had got lost or stifled on its way up the ladder. Right back in January 1963 she told the whole story, Profumo, Ivanov, warheads, reefers and all, to an ordinary policeman. He naturally arranged to go back and see her again in a day or two with colleagues from the Special

Branch (political and security police) and the Drug Squad. But
before this meeting could take place it was cancelled by the head
of the Special Branch. This left the ball in the court of the Criminal Investigation Department, but the head of that Department
followed suit and also cancelled the meeting, as far as his branch
was concerned, so that no full statement was ever taken.

But her short statement, the one made to the ordinary policeman, was on record. In the next ten days the head of the Security
Service on two separate occasions, and his deputy once, issued
firm negative instructions. Whatever their juniors might think,
Christine Keeler's story, or stories about her and Profumo, were
not to be further investigated (paras. 260–6). This part of Lord
Denning's report gives the impression of skating hurriedly or
perhaps incredulously over a rather tricky situation. The Security
Service had been lethargic, at the least. Paragraph 266 reads in
part:

On 7 February 1963, the Commander of Special Branch went to see
the Security Service with the report of the Marylebone officers of 5
February 1963. This report showed that the police had been told by
Christine Keeler on 26 January that there was an illicit association
between herself and Mr Profumo, that she had met Captain Ivanov on
a number of occasions, and that Stephen Ward had asked her to discover from Mr Profumo the date on which atomic secrets were to be
handed to Western Germany.... The matter was discussed by the
Commander of Special Branch with a senior officer of the Security
Service.... They decided that there was no security interest involved
such as to warrant any further steps being taken. The papers were put
before the Deputy Director-General, who agreed with the decision and
wrote his minute:

'No action on this at present. Please keep me informed of any
developments.'

In paragraph 210 the Security Service are reported as having
told the Prime Minister (this was after one of Harold Wilson's
letters to him) that: 'There is no truth in the story that the
Security Service was informed of the dates of, or anything else in
connexion with, Mr Profumo's alleged visits to Ward or to Miss
Keeler.' This was on 25 April. Paragraph 213 reads in part:

On Wednesday, 29 May 1963, the Head of the Security Service
reported to the Prime Minister and disclosed to him (what he and his

office had not known before) that 'in a statement which Christine Keeler made to the police in January 1963 she said that on one occasion, when she was going to meet Mr Profumo, Ward had asked her to discover from him the date on which certain atomic secrets were to be handed to West Germany by the Americans. It is understood that Miss Keeler denies having ever put such a question to Mr Profumo.'

It took four months for them to act. On the question whether the Security Service had known of Profumo's liaison with Christine Keeler back in 1961, Lord Denning had no doubt. Ward told him, as he had told his friends at the time and the public later, that he had told the Security Service about it while it was happening. The Security Service denied this. Lord Denning (paras. 34, 248, 259) reported that he was 'satisfied' that the Security Service did not know about it in 1961.

But the biggest surprise in the report was that everyone appeared to have forgotten who was in charge of Security at all. Denning unearthed an unpublished directive from the Home Secretary of 1952, saying it was the Home Secretary. But the Prime Minister always took questions about it in the House of Commons and, on the night when the five ministers sat up with Profumo drafting the statement, 'no one thought of asking the Home Secretary to stay'. The Lord Chancellor, in his private report earlier on, had not had the directive before him when he accepted that the Prime Minister was responsible for security. The Lord Chancellor had been wrong.

Denning's general conclusion was that the Security Service had not erred, but that the Government had.

The conduct of Mr Profumo was such as to create, amongst an influential section of the people, a reasonable belief that he had committed adultery with such a woman in such circumstances as the case discloses. It was the responsibility of the Prime Minister and his colleagues, and of them only, to deal with this situation: and they did not succeed in doing so.

On the night the Denning Report was published the Prime Minister once again lamented, this time on the radio, the enormity of the deceit which Profumo had practised; his voice was full of pure and passionate regret for the days before the Fall, when everyone had always been able to trust everyone.

CHAPTER 6

THE offence and disgrace of John Profumo seemed fair game compared with the ritual sacrifice of Stephen Ward. Probably few people really believed that he had told Christine Keeler classified facts which she then passed on to Ivanov. The picture was absurd: Christine Keeler rolled out from under saying, that was wonderful darling; now tell me about the warheads, and Ivanov rolled off from over saying, that was wonderful darling; now tell me what Jack said about the warheads. All this will be discussed in the next chapter. But the association with a girl who was also going with a Soviet diplomat was to say the least of it very bad politics, and Profumo deserved what he got, which was not the worst.

Ward, on the other hand, was dead, which he would not otherwise have been. The stories and wisecracks which had been going the rounds gave way at that time to fear. Some pristine conviction that whatever happened, in the last resort, England was all right deep down, and better than other places, was lost. A man, a silly man, no doubt, but a sane, and often happy, man had killed himself in transparent conviction of his own innocence and the guilt of others. Several intellectuals clubbed together to send a wreath to Ward's funeral, as to a victim. The *Guardian* said it was a bit of luck he had not been a mass murderer as well as everything else, and that the intellectuals must be Marxists encouraging corruption.

There are plenty of Wards around; there are two men still alive and unknown to the political public who make it their business to provide girls to important people. One of them works for a large industrial concern, and, whoever pays for the girls, it is not the clients. Ward had been living his life for years, at least since the end of the war, and it is important to see what sort of life that was. Burge, the counsel who defended him, told the jury that the key question was: did he do this for fun or for money?

For fun. He had a stable, swiftly changing, but always three or four on tap, of what 'society' people call *prettygirls*, pronouncing it all as one word. They were his, by an arrangement which suited all three parties, Ward, the girls, and 'society', but he was not paid for their use. No doubt he received favours which he would not otherwise have received – the nominal rent which Lord Astor arranged for him to pay the National Trust for the *cottage orné* was one such – but any idea of a pony a bash, as Ronna Ricardo said in one of the statements she withdrew, was from another world. His girls were *sortable*; they were true *demi-mondaines*. The arrangement suited 'society' because it saved them trouble; it suited the girls because it got them in touch with 'society', and it has proved possible to make very good indeed from being a Ward girl; and it suited Ward because he enjoyed it.

There was a need for him. There are always men who are used to getting things without working for them, and one of the things men like to get is girls. He was purveyor of milkmaids to top people. Probably there have always been such; when the earl married the milkmaid before the industrial revolution he may not always have found her himself. Certainly since, he has not had to. There is a class of public-school Tory who can best be understood by examining the prefix 'M'. 'M'tutor' is what Etonians call the intellectual lackeys to whom they are put out for education. The little labial derives from the eighteenth-century pronunciation 'me'; 'me father, me daughter, me butcher'. Etonians use it unselfconsciously for 'm'tutor' and will recognize it as a something relevant to them if you say 'm'tailor', 'm'toothmaker', or 'm'tractor', though they might not recognize 'm'procurer'. But, and here is the point, it would be impossible to say: 'M'battalion', 'm'company sergeant major', 'm'horse', or even 'm'dog'; these are things which are dignified by exposure to common risk with the master on the field of battle or the hunting field. If there is no risk of death or wounding together, the person used is expendable. If there is, the structure of romantic conservative loyalty, than which nothing in England is stronger, comes into play. Brigadier John Profumo is still alive.

Stephen Ward was not even a real doctor; he was a mere bone-setter, and, though commissioned, was so only as an officer stretcher-bearer. It is noticeable that most of the characters in this story had been in the Army (except Ivanov, who was from the other side and didn't count). Complete contempt for the inferior is only possible in armies where, if the troops won't fight, both officers and men can run away over open fields in their own time. If sailors won't fight, the officer sinks too. Therefore naval officers are careful not to feel contempt. It was Wellington who said: 'the scum of the earth'. Nelson used different language.

They deserted Ward with contempt. The judge himself remarked to the jury how strange it was that none of his powerful friends had come forward to help him in his hour of need, and told them they must not speculate about this. Others may. Lord Astor did not come forward. He is the present head of a family whose first founder, John Jacob Astor from Walldorf in Germany, showed such foresight in selling flutes to the American Indians and buying sections of Manhattan Island as to make work a matter of choice for his descendants, and not necessity. On the other hand that simple man and godly artist Stanley Spencer was fond of Lord Astor, and it was Astor's misfortune that he seemed to symbolize a whole class of people during this Affair. There still is, as there long has been in this country and many others, a fairly recognizable *set*, vacuous, aimless, vain, and insensitive, who live on their fellow men rather than with and for them. They are the buyers. (Work, on the whole, is not done, though it is possible for people with jobs to dissimulate their way into the set.) Where everything is bought, from private palaces to public images, then why not girls as well? Many were mentioned; many were not, but are well known to those who are in a position to see what makes England tick; many, no doubt, are not known at all. From Stephen Ward they had received much into their beds. The quickie, the short affair, the long affair, the special attention to special needs, and many, too, the wife. They could not get their own. Stephen provided.

But he also annoyed. There is more than craven fear of exposure and embarrassment in their silence. He served them, but he also hated them. Anyone who makes a life of purveying what is free for the asking may well despise his customers, and contempt is not far from hatred. He liked to see them squirm. He would promise this and that, and she would not turn up.

He put secret little signs on his portrait drawings. Selwyn Lloyd was punished for the pay pause with a tiny hammer and sickle behind his ear. Lucky Gordon, an obscure man, and one whose desserts are ambiguous, but not for that to be ruled out as a source of understanding, said at his trial that Stephen Ward liked to 'aggravate' people, and that he had taught Christine Keeler the knack. Ward was a sexual banana-skin merchant. Moreover, he hated conservatism. Not conservatives; they were his friends, or at least his *patrons* in a sense rich with mutual fear and contempt. But he regarded the doctrine of conservatism, or its practice, as something apt to destroy the life and soul of free men and women, as a dark threat to natural felicity, as evil in itself. He did better than he hoped for. And they killed him.

The name conservatism will survive; but it will not again mean the blatant purchase of that which should be built, enjoyed, loved, and celebrated – and the words fit whether we speak of sexual relationships or of city centres – as it did in 1963. The name *procurer* will survive, but it will not again mean Stephen Ward.

The other characters in the ritual seem flat and small beside the silly great scapegoat himself. John Profumo could just as well have been anyone else. The Fifth Baron of the Kingdom of the Two Sicilies concealed an immigrant origin like another. His father and grandfather built up an insurance connexion which left the third generation nothing to worry about. There was no reason to think him good at anything, and no reason to think him especially bad. Any other rich young man of engaging temperament and moderate ability could no doubt have become the youngest member of Parliament at a wartime by-election, have called attention to himself by supporting General MacArthur in his desire to use nuclear weapons in Korea, and thus in time, given the long hegemony of a party and a general spirit to which engaging temperament and moderate ability were sufficient, have become Secretary of State for War. His tenure of that office was in political terms accurately described by George Wigg. He was there to adjust the manpower target and the recruitment results to each other in a manner which neither shocked public opinion nor made necessary the re-introduction of conscription. He had done it quite well for a time, and would no doubt have been given larger chores. If he had indeed been destined for promotion he would have had to move at about that time in any case; the recruiting figures were just beginning to slump again.

Christine Keeler did not make a very grand impression in court. She was there to protect what Italian witnesses call '*la mia verità*,' 'my truth', as opposed to anyone else's, and for her this was that she was not a whore. Stephen Ward had told her that as long as there was some real affection, some real relationship, however slight, money might correctly pass. If one was not entirely a thing in one's own eyes, and in the man's, it was not prostitution. These are old problems, much discussed even before the Restoration Dramatists, and even since Bernard Shaw. Ward was not a guide richly qualified by disinterest, and she had not gone too far into the matter.

Some purported memoirs of Johnny Edgecombe's were published in continental weeklies during the early summer of 1963,* and they gave a vivid account of her way of life. Here was someone who filled highly divergent bills; someone who could be rough to the smooth, and smooth to the rough: a sort of social equalizer in the world of sexual endeavour. So much Edgecombe said. At the Old Bailey she repeated a line which she had used to the police, and in the Magistrate's Court, and which had already been all over the headlines: Stephen Ward 'had full control over my mind'. She illustrated the word *mind* by laying her fingers on her belly, not flat, as if it belonged to her, but pointed fastidiously in from a wrist held far forward, as one might indicate something one really did not much care for at all.

Mandy Rice-Davies, being extremely young, astonished the nation by not being what one would expect a whore to be, even a successful one. Shameless she surely was, and to those for whom all shameless girls are whores, she must have filled the bill very nicely. But confused, oppressed, depressed, or spiritually corrupt, as others would have expected, she was not. She had only to laugh when the judge told her it was not a laughing matter that Stephen Ward should be in the next room while she was in bed with a man, for everyone to wonder how many rooms away the next nearest person has to be in the experience of judges before one can relax. She had only to tell

*e.g. *Confessioni Stop*, Milan, Nos. 770 and 771

Ward's defence counsel that she had not named Douglas Fairbanks because she hoped to get more money for her story from the Press, but because she didn't like him, for a money-loving and impulse-fearing society to gasp with admiration. She had only to have herself photographed making ten funny faces for a German weekly to show all those who saw it in spite of the libel laws which prevented its distribution that people, especially if they are young enough, can survive whoring for a bit.

But even she tried to kill herself. She said it was for grief that her boyfriend Rachman was dead. Stephen Ward said that it was because he had not left her any money.

Ronna Ricardo and Vicky Barrett would not have been used to doing or saying things because they were true, or even 'their truth'; a person who has been formed by the habit of doing what someone else wants and pretending to like it may easily be put into court determined to give false evidence, but cannot well be relied upon to maintain it.

CHAPTER 7

THE political texture and continuity of a society runs in two dimensions. There is, as it were, the geographical dimension, which is its institutions: its parliament, its cabinet or central committee of the party, its courts, armed forces, police, educational establishments, social classes, and so on and so on. The second dimension is the temporal one; it comprises all the events and processes. It comprises both the continuous processes, the movements of the market up and down, the slow swings of franchise and opinion and the corresponding shifts of political power, the decade-long tendencies to this or that form or custom, and also (which concerns us here) the short sharp events, the convulsive movements, the extra-curricular phenomena of politics.

The greatest of these is the revolution, when a whole society heaves up, typically with bloodshed, and settles again into a different shape. But at a lower level than this, and sometimes involving no permanent change in the shape of society, are various types of short sharp political events which may, if they become acute, exercise some of the purgative and disruptive functions of a revolution. They are the crisis, the scandal, and the affair. A domestic crisis is purely political in nature; the government has done something which loses it the confidence of a sector of society, or of a greater sector than usual, and the question arises whether it would not be better to have a change. The scandal is purely personal: a minister or other highly-placed person does something in his private life which is felt to unfit him for his high place. The affair is a mixture; it is scandal and crisis together. In recent English history there were crises in 1940, when Churchill superseded Chamberlain on political grounds, and in 1956 when Macmillan superseded Eden on political grounds. There were scandals when Parnell, the leader of the Irish members of Parliament at Westminster, was forced out of public life for adultery, and when the same thing happened to Sir Charles Dilke. These were major scandals, when powerful and significant men were publicly broken for private conduct. In recent years there have been many minor scandals, when less powerful and significant politicians have been broken for private conduct, often for the suspicion or the certainty of homosexual behaviour.

The affair has been a normal part of the constitutions of certain European countries for many years, particularly of France and Italy. It is in a sense a little revolution, and flourishes best in states with a revolutionary tradition. The prototype of the modern affair was the Dreyfus Affair in France (around 1900) when a Jewish army officer was accused by an anti-semitic officer caste of selling secrets to a hostile power and was vindicated after some years, largely by the eloquence and diligence of the novelist Émile Zola. The affair was about scapegoats, about lying, about national security, about race.

The only other affair which has reached anything like these proportions (though the Profumo Affair looks like doing so in time) was perhaps the Montesi Affair in Italy (1954–8) where the son of the Foreign Minister came under suspicion of having done away with a carpenter's daughter at an orgy, and was finally exonerated, by absence of evidence, though not before countless other reputations had been, many of them rightly, ruined.

It had been about lying, about debauchery, about class, about official covering-up.

Other recent affairs have included the Van Doren Affair in the United States (1960), when a well-informed young man from a family of New England Brahmins had cheated on a TV quiz programme, being fed the answers in advance. It brought television down to the level of the Press in popular estimation; hitherto it had enjoyed, because newer, a sort of glamour the Press had long since lost. The affair was about lying and about class; but it differed in not involving Government.

The Affair of the *Ballets Roses* in France (1959) was hardly an affair at all, being scarcely more than a scandal. The President of the National Assembly and some other important people used to go to a suburban villa to watch erotic dancing and exhibitions, including under-age girls. It was about debauchery.

The Spiegel Affair in Germany (1962) arose when the Hamburg weekly *Der Spiegel* (The Mirror) published some confidential assessments of the efficiency of the German Army and some other results of a NATO exercise called Fallex 62, tending to show how very many civilian casualties there would be in a nuclear war in Europe. The Defence Minister, Strauss, had several of the *Spiegel* journalists tried and imprisoned and had one of them forcibly returned to Germany by the German military attaché in Madrid. He several times denied the Madrid bit in the Bundestag, but was finally forced to admit it, and so lost his job. He did not lose his following among the Christian Democrats of Bavaria, nor his prospects. The Affair was about lying, about the misuse of the judiciary, about official covering-up, about defence policy, and about militarism, since it is militaristic to conceal from a population how many of them would be killed if there was a war.

In Britain, on the other hand, the Affair is something rather new. We have had a royal affair in this century; the abdication of King Edward VIII.

This was a fully-fledged affair; the private wish of the King to marry a divorced woman, Mrs Simpson, led to public battles in the Press and in conversation, to the lining up of forces more or less conscious of their identity, to accusations of bad faith, obscurantism, immoralism, and all the rest of it, and to the general sense of national upheaval which distinguishes a true affair from a mere scandal or a crisis. But it was a one-man affair; the ink was used and the air heated for one question only; what is it proper for a king to do? The individual citizen might up to a point identify himself with his monarch, but only in the abstract, only anthropologically.

The Profumo Affair ramified. It had almost all the usual ingredients: national security, debauchery, lying, race, class, covering-up. So many, and, in a way, such ordinary, people were involved. Profumo himself, a slick, cheerful Tory in-grouper, bought a girl. How many men of his age and class did not see themselves as slick, cheerful Tory in-groupers, and how many had not bought a girl? Christine Keeler, a pretty girl from the suburbs, came to the big city and went from bad to worse. The nightmare of how many parents?

The political effect of the Affair stems largely from Profumo's actions and, if we are to learn anything from it, they must be examined and related to our standards and customs. It is not enjoyable for the pamphleteer to pick up the acts of a fellow citizen in ethical or sociological forceps and declare them to be right or wrong, venial or grave. This would only be enjoyable if the fellow citizen were either guiltless, or, though guilty, the personal enemy of the pamphleteer. Profumo is neither of those things.

He had a liaison with Christine Keeler, who also had a liaison with Ivanov, he paid her, and he lied to the House of Commons about it. His actions must therefore be considered under the three headings of prostitution, espionage, and mendacity.

Prostitution, in British law, is when a woman sells her body for the purposes of sexual intercourse or acts of lewdness. It sounds awful, and almost everybody is against it in theory. Most women and a good many men also make a point of not doing it in practice. But there is nothing black and white about it. In our culture, the function of prostitution is mainly exercised by professionals, who live by it. It is reprobated, and paid. In others, these things are ordered differently. In some, it is paid but not reprobated. In some it is not even specialized, and any wife or sister or daughter will undertake a ritual act of prostitution for the sake of a visitor's goodwill or divine approval, or the fertility of herd and crop.

But in England now, the function of prostitution lies at one of the richest intersections of money and 'morals'. We whip the whore in our speeches, we put her ponce in the stocks of punitive legislation, we hound a borderline character like Stephen Ward to his death, but equally we use the whore till she's unfit for anything else, and pay her up to £50 a night for it. Many individuals are not hyprocrites about this; they dignify either their condemnation by abstention, or their indulgence by tolerance. But our society as a whole is majestically hypocritical; the way it combines condemnation with indulgence is known all over the world.

This does not matter too much. All societies and nations, and all the sub-cultures which make them up, have zones of hypocrisy where it has proved impossible to bring standards and actions within shouting distance of one another, and where many do the thing they condemn. This situation is in itself satisfying: it would not continue if it were not.

Societies without prostitution do exist; one has been described in lucid depth by Dr Verrier Elwin in his book *The Muria and their Ghotul*.* This Indian people, some neighbouring ones, and some peoples elsewhere in Asia and Africa are able to do without prostitution in later life because all the children have lived away from the grown-ups in a separate teenagers' pavilion called a Ghotul. Here, from as soon as they are able until the age of marriage, which in the case of the Muria is about seventeen, they live in total promiscuity. After that they marry and, though divorce is permitted, their divorce rate is a tiny fraction of ours, and prostitution is unknown. The evidence that the hypocrisy surrounding prostitution in our culture is in itself satisfying is that the enemies of prostitution, instead of studying and probably commending adolescent promiscuity, generally condemn that as strongly as the prostitution to which it appears to be the alternative. The Christian objection to prostitution has not changed its ground in two thousand years; reformers who really wish to get something done are normally reluctant to wait so long.

We should, therefore, accept prostitution as a requisite part of the emotional and moral balance of our society, and of almost all other societies around us. We, as a society, want it that way, and our secular licence to cry out in objection is dearer to us than the idea of a prostitution-free society, which we could probably achieve if we wished.

This being so, we must next consider what part in prostitution we would wish to allow to different sorts of citizens. It is obvious that if the Archbishop of Canterbury is caught whoring there will be a great scandal, but if a building labourer is, there will be none. To posit the extremes of the permissibility scale as regards the agent is already to see the nature of our usual judgements. If the Archbishop goes whoring, he is a damned bad Archbishop. He preaches chastity, and it is as much a part of the customary balance of our society that chastity should be preached as that prostitution should be practised. Just as the prostitute is for practising prostitution, so the Archbishop is for condemning it, and we shall never abolish either alone, though we might abolish both together. The building labourer is in a different situation; he may either preach or practise either chastity or

*O.U.P., 1947

95

unchastity without in the least affecting his usefulness as a building labourer. We don't care what he does, and he does not expect us to. But the in-between men? The general manager of the industrial firm? The doctor? The psychiatrist? The mayor? The Member of Parliament? The university professor? The leader, in this sphere or that?

One can only ask: does it impede his proper function? Bishop – yes. Labourer – no. Secretary of State for War?

The Secretary of State for War, in theory, is hired by the rest of us to order the Army in accordance with the wishes of the people as expressed through Parliament. In practice he will look after the Army according not solely to the wishes of the people, but to some other factors as well. But he is there only to look after the Army. He may be a good Minister, or a bad one; this will depend in the first place on the usual list of political qualities. Is he a good administrator? A sensitive interpreter of general mood? An efficient politician, so that things actually get done when they need to be? Can he reconcile conflicting interests, see the way through tangles, make a good speech, foster the useful, calm the agitated, sidetrack the useless, sterilize the destructive? When these capacities are to be exercised in a field, such as Army affairs, to which prostitution is irrelevant, the fact that he goes whoring may in itself appear irrelevant too.

The sex life of a Minister or other public man (not being a preacher) is not in itself a proper subject for public interest. He may, as far as the action itself goes, find his deepest satisfaction in dressing himself and half a dozen companions in masonic aprons and tying up duck-billed platypuses with red ribbons in front of six-way mirrors without affecting his ability to improve recruiting or develop new radio-telephony sets for the Army of the Rhine.

That is how it is, or more precisely how it could be in a society which knew how to keep things separate. But this we rather conspicuously do not know. The objection of many people to the very idea of such goings on means that, if it becomes known that he does this sort of thing, blackmailers may use this knowledge to extract money from him, which will worry him and thus make him less efficient. More than this, they may seek larger advantages for themselves or their friends,

96

such as contracts here or there (the War Office is a big buying department) or even, as they did from the humbler Vassall, secrets for hostile foreign powers.

And how much less than masonic platypuses opens the Minister to blackmail? A long-standing affair with a woman other than his wife? Hardly. A short affair? Conceivably. It depends on the man's relations with his wife. Most politicians now would probably not rate the continued deception of their wives a higher good than uncorrupt administration. But once bring payment into the sexual relation and you get to trickier ground. The public revelation that the Rt Hon X had had a whore and paid her would offend not only his wife, but broad sectors of the people at large, and he would thus in theory pay a higher price to prevent it. Moreover, to get blackmailed is in itself a disgrace to many people; 'at least he could have had the decency not to get caught'.

Repeated purchase of whores, as a pattern of life, would in theory necessitate a higher price still, and thus be the more blameworthy on grounds of the general discretion which is needed for decent administration.

And so on through straightforward whoremongering to harmless kinks and away into the mists of the behaviour we necessarily make criminal ... violence, the white drugs. The blackmailers' leverage naturally becomes greater at each step, but in time the calculation becomes unreal. No white drug addict could be Secretary of State for War anyhow.

The feeling that we want ministers to be personally and sexually *good*, at least as good as us and probably better, may be due to the fact that divorce between church and state is still pending. The Queen is still head of both, the bishops still sit in Parliament, the legislative assemblies of the Church cannot change religious ritual, only those of the state can, and so forth. England is not, and never has been, a lay state in the full sense that France or America have been for a century and a half.

This being so, a certain religious flavour naturally hangs still about those who advise the man who appoints the bishops, just as a highly political flavour still hangs about some of the bishops.

Perhaps for this reason by far the greatest volume of Press comment generated by the Profumo Affair has been about sexual morals, and by far the greater part of that has been shocked, restrictionist, even demanding what the *British Weekly*, the Church of Scotland paper, called 'a national act of cleansing and commitment that will lead Britain out of this mess to find a new purpose under God in the world and for the world'. 'Thus fell Rome,' headlined the *New Daily*: 'Corruption, Degeneracy, and Indolence in High Places.' *The Times*, as we have noticed, mentioned blood, sweat, toil, and tears. Dr Donald Soper, away to the left in *Tribune*, wrote: 'If our fathers were persuaded to behave themselves for fear of going to hell, their children have a much more immediate reason for personal discipline – indifference to it is a mortal danger to everybody on earth.' A statement read out at all the masses one Sunday in Westminster Cathedral said: 'We feel . . . that it is our duty to warn our people to be on their guard lest any sensational reporting of these matters, whether by Press, radio, or television, should in itself prove a source of scandal and even moral temptation to impressionable young people.'

These feelings are part, no doubt, of what the *British Weekly*, in the same leader, called 'the solidarity of sin'. There are some people who feel, perhaps because of their own undigested wish to have done likewise, that if others sin they themselves are guilty. The incontinence of Profumo means a loss of vital fluid to the whole nation; the feeling shows in fossil form the Victorian belief that orgasm is debilitating, a belief appropriate to a mercantile and mechanical civilization, as though men were banks, liable to runs, or boilers, liable to leaks. This particular temperament, since it can by definition never be at peace with itself, is for ever restlessly writing to the Press, or even editing it.

But of those who were polled early in June about which was the most important, security, lies in Parliament, or the private morals of Ministers, only 13.3 per cent answered: the private morals of Ministers. An inquiry carried out in Profumo's own constituency by the *Banbury Guardian*, found that there too, though his lie was resented, his affair with Christine Keeler was not.

Before proceeding to the topic of espionage, it may be convenient to digress and speak of drug addiction. Christine Keeler smoked hemp, and said Stephen Ward had introduced her to it. This he denied with fervour in court, saying he had lectured and written to *The Times* on its dangers. The undoubted fact that hemp is more easily obtainable in London now than it used to be, and is used especially by young people, gave rise to many sensational and even apocalyptic articles in the Press.

Indian hemp, or marijuana (the Spanish form of the Arabic word *mahjnoun*), can be both eaten and smoked. The effects are rather similar to those of alcohol. It is not related either in origin or effects to the powerful drugs, opium, cocaine, morphine, or heroin.

In North Africa, among the Arabs of Tunisia, Algeria, and Morocco, marijuana is the normal stimulant, just as alcohol is to us; alcohol is forbidden and regarded as a sign of degeneracy, just as marijuana is by us. To the great majority of the people, marijuana is the normal thing to take after the evening meal, and at parties. Its effects seem just what those of alcohol are to us; it makes people happy or melancholy, talkative or maudlin, according to temperament. Some have hangovers, some don't seem to. It is not aphrodisiac in general, perhaps rather less than alcohol. It does not produce trance or hallucinations, though it does produce some odd and rather delightful effects, especially visual, in large doses. It does not seem to lead to addiction more easily than alcohol; illness, whether mental or physical, will no doubt predispose to addiction in both cases. Most European travellers probably return from the Muslim weed to the Christian juice with some relief, perhaps owing to cultural conditioning. It is important for public opinion to realize that our horror of hemp in England now is an ignorant one. The last White Paper on *Drug Addiction* (1961) says roundly: 'In our view cannabis' (the botanical name for hemp) 'is not a drug of addiction', but addiction to alcohol in Britain 'is a serious problem'. A lot of suffering could be avoided among older people who know their children smoke hemp if the law were changed to take account of the facts in this field, and if the popular Press would tell the truth as set out in this White Paper.

*

If the relationship between Profumo and Christine Keeler had been between them alone it is likely no more would ever have been heard of it, and that most people, if asked, would not have wished to hear of it. It is certain that plenty of other Ministers, both in the Conservative Government of 1963 and in former ones, have had relationships like that with girls like that, and with less attractive and educated girls, and that they will continue to do so in future governments. Only itchy prudes will worry about this. But once introduce Ivanov, and the picture changes. What was feared, or what it was purported was feared, was that Profumo told Christine Keeler things which she then passed on to Ivanov, or even that he told them direct to Ivanov, and that they were things which it would have been useful for the Soviet Union to know in the cold war, or even in a hot one.

The only question which it had ever been publicly alleged she was asked to ask Profumo, 'the date the Americans would give nuclear warheads to West Germany', is a nonsense. Allen Dulles, the retired head of the American Central Intelligence Agency, said in an interview that it would not be 'a very penetrating intelligence question to ask', and that is indeed so. Nuclear warheads have been on West German soil, under the control of American soldiers, for several years now. Some delivery vehicles, Honest John and Mace rockets for the most part, but more recently also the longer range Pershing rockets, have been for some years under West German control. If the warheads were to pass from American control to German, there would have to be a revision of the Macmahon Act, which was made by the United States Congress precisely to prohibit such devolution of control to allies. This revision would take place in a blaze of publicity. All through the time when Christine Keeler was alleged to have been asked to ask this, various changes in basic Western strategy were being openly discussed which would have required precisely such a revision, and the devolution of control of nuclear weapons to America's continental allies. Those who thought this should be done, though not numerous or powerful, were articulate, and so of course were the majority who backed the policy of those days (which is still the policy), namely that it should not be done. The relevant journals and newspapers were full of the great debate, and Russian diplomats in the West took a lively and unconcealed interest in it. They would no more have had to put a spy in the War Minister's bed to find out, than they would have had to photograph secret files to find out if Britain proposed to adopt a decimal currency.

On the other hand it is possible that Stephen Ward had been asked to ask her to ask as a testing question, to find out if the line Ward-Keeler-Profumo would carry a real intelligence load later. Indeed, Lord Denning reported that Ivanov had asked Ward to ask this question of 'his influential friends' in general. Though not indeed a penetrating intelligence question, it would not be a stupid test question. If the answer had come back: 'March next year,' or something like that, the Soviet Intelligence Service would have known one of the amateurs along the line was making it up, and they would have discarded the line. If the answer had come back: 'It's not like that at all,' or 'not while I'm around', they could have gone one step further in testing it out.

This is speculation. But there is no doubt that Ward told his friends he had been in contact with a Mr Woods of the Security Service, had been advised to keep in touch with Ivanov, and had even asked Ivanov questions for, as he believed, the Foreign Office.

What is certain is that the triangle Profumo-Keeler-Ivanov laid Profumo wide open to blackmail. The scandal which broke when it was finally discovered, and the degree of ruin which overtook him personally, can hardly have surprised Profumo. The extent to which he expected them is the measure of his vulnerability to blackmail. In the market of these things, big scandal equals big hush payment, and big hush payment may be made in big secrets. We should probably know if Profumo had been unsuccessfully blackmailed by the Russian Intelligence Service; he would probably tell us about it if he had stood up to them. But we do not know, and we shall never know, whether he was successfully blackmailed in the nineteen months between August 1961 and March 1963; we only know that the Russians had good leverage on him. And in the eleven weeks between March and June 1963 the good leverage was doubled by his public lie. Harold Wilson's phrase 'we shall never know' is not just politically convenient rhetoric. It cannot be assumed that a man who has lied in order to conceal adultery from the House of Commons will not lie in order to conceal a breach of security from Lord Denning, any more than it can be assumed that he will. The only other people who would know are the Soviet Intelligence Service, because when you have a real hold over a man there is no longer any reason to complicate the channel with cut-outs, whether conscious or unconscious.

So much for the risk of a breach of security: the risk was high. But when such a breach occurs, what does it mean for the rest of us? Does it for instance increase the risk of war, or of defeat in war? In these security scandals, the public is never told what sort of information is at stake. Spy after spy is caught and punished, or not caught, but identified after he has skipped to the other side. What information have they passed across? What information could they have passed across? When they skip, it is of course impossible for the Government to know what they have passed. But when they are caught, they presumably tell.

In the absence of information, feeling runs high. There are those who feel that if the Russians see a list of spare parts for rifles marked 'confidential' then democracy is doomed. Others, exemplified by the novelist Naomi Mitchison, who wrote to the *Guardian* during the Profumo Affair, believe Secretaries of State for War don't know anything anyhow.

The shape of the intelligence war between the Soviet bloc and the Western bloc has been determined since the Second World War by the often-noticed fact that they are a closed society, and we are an open one. There are many things we like to know about each other which are secret in the East, and open in the West. Among such things are major political objectives, economic statistics, economic conditions, local grievances, troop and shipping movements, the deployment and composition of military units, the locality of strategic missile sites, the numbers of weapons in given categories, and their broad performance characteristics. All these the Russians can find out about us by reading our newspapers, and occasionally hiring a car and going for a drive. The only way we can find out those things about them is by sending in secret agents, or cracking cyphers, or tapping phones, or building fantastically expensive and complicated pieces of machinery to go in aeroplanes and satellites. The

Russians can of course do these things too, but they do not have to waste them on finding out any of the things listed above; they can devote all their resources to the remaining target subjects, which are equally secret on both sides.

These are: immediate plans and policy. The line Western negotiators will take next week, whether or not troops will be sent to a place in the Middle or Far East, the vote to be cast in the U.N., the intention to declare a particular diplomat *persona non grata*. All such things which are to be done within a few days or at most weeks are kept secret in the West, and will thus become objects of clandestine intelligence. A correct report will enable the Eastern negotiators to prepare an advantageous position in the negotiations, to send, or refrain from sending, troops to match ours, to levy, or not to bother to levy, votes against ours in the U.N., to enable the diplomat to leave before he can be expelled, or to expel one of ours first.

Also secret in the West are the detailed performance characteristics of our weapons systems. Example: will the French Mirage IV bomber fly to Warsaw and back after refuelling in flight, or to Moscow and back, or to Irkutsk one way, or only to Warsaw one way?

The question is not of much interest to the Polish Government; it gets there anyhow. But it is of some interest to the Soviet Government. Not because the *Force de Frappe* is very terrifying compared with the American or even the British forces, but because it is controlled by someone quite different, who might use it in quite different circumstances. They know it is going to be a force of fifty or sixty atomic bombers, later carrying thermo-nuclear bombs. But if they want to find out how far it can hit, they must engage in clandestine intelligence.

The same with penetration aids. What kind of radar waves, in what circumstances, are we in the West capable of bending away or flicking off? On the answer to this question depends the useful or the wasted deployment of very much money and effort in the Soviet programme of research and development for defensive radar.

And on a more humdrum level too. Was it really true that a large proportion of the British troops sent to Kuwait passed out from heatstroke, as George Wigg said? Should the Russians advise their friends in Asia that they could safely ignore British troops who had come straight out from Salisbury Plain, because they would be laid out, and only worry about those who had come from Kenya or Cyprus, where it is already rather hot? How many men, from places how hot?

There is indeed much that a Soviet spy could usefully try to find out.

The immediate impulse of the general public is, and is strongly, to take what steps can be taken to prevent his finding out. It is a useful impulse, but probably not for the first reason that comes into one's mind. If the Russians do penetrate our secrets in these matters, they will certainly take whatever steps appear to them advantageous (or as they would say, 'correct'), and these will usually (though not always) be to our disadvantage. If they do not, they will still have to take some steps in the field concerned, and these steps may be to our advantage, or they may be to our disadvantage. If they cannot find out how many troops we intend to send, they may send great fleets and armies which will upset a whole corner of the globe which we had intended to leave alone. If they cannot find out whether a Soviet diplomat is to be expelled, they may expel a Western one just in case, and thereby *start* an expulsion battle. If they cannot find out how far the Mirage IV will fly, they may prepare a great strike on French airfields, a preparation which is quite unnecessary to their security and which, being detected by American intelligence, may give rise to unfounded fears of a local aggression in Western Europe. If they cannot find out how many British soldiers were laid out by heatstroke, they may be tempted to send in Russian 'volunteers' in case none had been.

The actual military and political harm which may be done to a country these days by bad security is probably easy to over-estimate. In 1959 and 1960, U.S. Intelligence estimated that there was, or soon would be, a 'missile gap'–i.e. that the Russians were, or would soon be, ahead in numbers of missiles. America therefore raced to outbuild, as she thought, and arrived at her present dangerous and destabilizing superiority. There never was a missile gap: the mistake arose because scrappy intelligence data was interpreted by fearful persons and militarists in a pessimistic manner. If there had been no intelligence data the entire American economy might well have been turned on to making missiles. If there had been good intelligence data, in other words, if the Russians had had bad security, the world might have been a safer place today, both for them and for us. And, of course, this works the other way round too.

Before the alleged missile gap there had been the alleged bomber gap. Earlier in the 1950s the U.S. Intelligence estimate was that the Soviet Union could, and therefore certainly would, build a great many inter-continental bombers. The U.S. therefore built a great many inter-continental bombers, and ended up with far more than the Soviet Union. The U.S. superiority in both bombers and missiles at this time has led the Soviet Union to live in continual fear, itself in part the result of imperfect intelligence, that the U.S. was contemplating a first-strike nuclear war. This has made them intensely secretive about the locality of their own strategic bases, which would have to be hit in such a first strike, and thereby increased American suspicion of their motives.

As this goes to Press, it seems as though the conventional gap with which Western military planners and politicians have lived for years, that is, the superiority of Eastern conventional forces on the ground in Europe, may turn out to have been as much of a chimera as the bomber and missile gaps which preceded it. Strong interests were acting on the American government to overestimate Soviet bomber and missile strength; the overestimate enabled the U.S. Air Force and arms industry to wax rich and powerful. The motive for exaggerating Eastern land forces, if indeed there has been an exaggeration, is not so clear. It may have been to encourage America's European allies to increase the number of their conventional forces, and the line may now be being changed because their continued reluctance to do so had led some of them, and especially West Germany, to rely very heavily on the early use of nuclear weapons in a war, a strategy which the U.S., with its greater experience of the things, now sees to be dangerous.

Enough has been said to show that good security, which equals bad intelligence, is not always or necessarily a stabilizing factor in the world. If I tell my enemy nothing, and prevent his finding out, it may make me safer or it may not.

Like so much else in the world now, secrecy was good when nations could hope to win wars. The nation state is that which goes to war and hopes to win, but now that it cannot, it is fast losing its significance. We retain armies, and secretaries of state for war to control them. It is never advisable for the secretaries of state for war, or anyone else, to pass secrets to possible enemy states; not only because to do so may still make war or limited defeat more likely, but also because it reinforces the sentiment of nationhood to have in the midst of the nation one who would have been an undoubted killer of his own men a hundred years ago. The more that sentiment is reinforced, the slower will be the transition to a world system which will give the peoples a better chance of survival than the present one.

Espionage and security (in the sense of national secrecy) are part of the traditional world of nation-states in which we still live, but out of which most of us can now see into an alternative system. The process of making this transition will last a generation or two yet, and every time there comes a convulsion of *national* sentiment, whether it is to flog the uppish wog, or to take vengeance on the leaky vessel, or anything else, the process is delayed and our precarious stability endangered.

These long-term considerations make it inadvisable for ministers to pass secrets; but there are short-term considerations too. In a situation where information is restricted – and we shall live in that situation for many decades yet before the nation-state fades away – in such a situation, military and other sensitive information must be passed to potentially hostile states, when it is passed at all, in a controlled manner and so as to further reasonable objectives. It may occasionally be useful, necessary, or even vital to let a potential enemy know something which is usually kept secret. An example would be if the Russians came mistakenly to believe that we were going to send forces into E. Germany to 'liberate' it. In those circumstances, it might be most desirable purposely to leak to them valid documents showing how our mobile forces were in fact scheduled to be employed for the next few months. What must be prevented from happening is that secrets should be passed across all higgledy-piggledy, without control, and in such a way that no one knows what the other side knows about us and what it doesn't. And this situation can arise more quickly when the top man is blackmailed than when an underling is.

Lastly, and perhaps worst, there was the lie to Parliament. Our sort of democracy rests on the principles of free election, supremacy of legislature, free information. We choose the men we want; in Parliament they have the power to do what they think we want; and they are entitled to know the truth about what is happening, since only thus will they be able to see that what happens is what we want to happen. Profumo denied Parliament the last of these three principles; for eleven weeks they believed (or did not believe, according to temperament and other complex factors) that the Secretary of State for War had not (for what that was worth, considering security and other complicated factors) gone to bed with Christine Keeler.

If, as happens in the Soviet Union, we are not free to elect which men we want to a sovereign parliament, whatever Parliament there is can be no more than an organ of academic discussion within licensed limits.

If, as happens in Gaullist France, Parliament is not free to make the laws it wishes and choose the minister in whom it has confidence, that Parliament is no more than a collection of advisors on accountancy. If, as Britain risks by the appointment of Conservative Ministers, Parliament is not told the truth, Parliament becomes a party of important sheep leading a larger party of unimportant sheep in any direction chosen by the man to whom it has given its confidence in what may or may not have been a true understanding of his character and attitudes. Parliament exists to be told the truth to.

It has never been wholly told the truth to, but not even their staunchest friends could claim that Macmillan's Government had improved on the situation as they found it. Convenience has many times been put before truth. It was inconvenient that certain politicians should be at liberty in Nyasaland while the Government were trying to bash the heads of three territories together into a Central African Federation, contrary to the long and forcefully expressed wish of the people who lived there. They therefore invented a massacre plot to justify their imprisonment. Outcry in England led to the appointment of an inquiry which reported that there had been no massacre plot. Parliament had not been told the truth when it was claimed that there had been. A Nigerian politician called Enahoro was returned to Nigeria for trial on charges of treason, and the Government told the Parliament that the Nigerian Government had promised that he would be allowed to have whatever lawyer he chose for his defence. He was not allowed the lawyer of his choice: when it was told that he would be, the Parliament had not been told the truth. A missile called Skybolt, under development in the U.S., was to provide the next few years of the independent British nuclear deterrent. The Government repeatedly told Parliament that there was no reason to suppose the American development project would be cancelled, but it was cancelled, and a senior British officer who had been responsible for talking to the Americans about it during that time said in print that he could not remember a meeting when the Americans had not warned him that it might be cancelled. The Parliament had not been told the truth.

There are plenty of other examples. One should not be surprised or indignant about it; there are certain sorts of policies which can only be sustained by lying to Parliament, and the Conservative Government was committed to several of them. You can do it for a while, and more and more people will begin to have the reaction: 'well, of course they lie; it's what they're for, isn't it?' – and for a long time no one cares. In some countries, under some political systems, they never care again, and that country becomes a corrupt tyranny. In others, including, happily, this one, they suddenly start caring again before it is too late. That is one of the things that happened during the Profumo affair. We may be grateful that the British people was still capable of caring for truth, but we cannot be grateful to a government who put them to the test.

And so there was a great scandal; everybody cared very much, and the proceedings were subjected to voluminous but imprecise scrutiny in several criminal trials, in Parliament and the Press, and in the Denning Report. The basic claim of the Government was that Profumo had deceived everybody, that this was very regrettable, and that there is no defence against a determined liar. The liar had been sacrificed, and a bigger undesirable yet, Stephen Ward, had been tried and found guilty, and had killed himself. Thus everything was all right. But on the morrow of the publication of the Denning Report, it seemed as though people would continue to worry about these two aspects: the long credit given to Profumo's lie, and the conviction of Stephen Ward. Denning left so much unanswered: not, no doubt, because he meant to, but because being a judge, that is, formed in the very heart of the English establishment, he could not see how much more there was that needed to be answered.

An entirely detached inquirer would surely have asked the following questions, and insisted on answers. Johnny Edgecombe was tried and convicted for having shot at Christine Keeler, without her having been there to give evidence. How often in recent years has the prosecution agreed to prosecute a man for shooting at someone when the someone, still very much alive, was not called to give evidence?

Ward said he had told the Security Service about the Profumo-Keeler-Ivanov triangle back in 1961. He told enough people about it then for it to appear in 'joke' form in the Press in August 1962, in the *Queen* feature with which I opened this book. He told the public and the jury at his own trial that he had told the Security Service. The Security Service denied knowing anything about it until at least January 1963 and possibly (for the minute to the Prime Minister of 25 April quoted on p. 83 above could bear this interpretation) they denied knowing anything about it until 29 May 1963. (Nor does Lord Denning's presentation of this minute do anything to clear up the obscurity.) And indeed how could one be sure that Ward was lying and the Security Service, or individuals in it, were not? Was Ward 'a liar'? He lied once during this Affair in order to back up his friend Profumo's lie, but not otherwise, as far as can be seen from Denning's Report. What would his motive for lying on this occasion be? What would a Security Service officer's motive for lying be?

Lord Denning held the Security Service not to have erred, and explained the way they sat on the story in January 1963 by saying that by that date it was a matter of the 'moral misbehaviour of a minister', and no longer a security risk. It was not a security risk because Ivanov had already left the country. This reasoning seems defective. Either the link between Profumo and Ivanov had never been a security risk at all, or the possibility of Profumo's doing something like that again made him a security risk as long as he held office, irrespective of one particular Ivanov's having left the country. What were the reactions of the Security Service to this argument? Was it put to them?

Lord Denning held that the Government had been wrong to act simply on their belief that Profumo was telling the truth; they ought to have acted on the assumption that though they believed him nobody else would. This seems a long way round; why should they have believed him at all? Did Lord Denning consider the personal histories of the ministers who drafted Profumo's lying statement for him, and so resolutely refrained from inquiring again whether the facts were as he stated them? Did he know that the Attorney General had been at the same school (Harrow), the same college (Brasenose, Oxford), and in the same regiment during the war (Northamptonshire Yeomanry) as Profumo? Did he know that Deedes had been at the same school? Did he ask either of these men whether they had ever had occasion to doubt Profumo's word before? Or whether his having met and liked a girl like Christine Keeler without making love was in accordance with what they knew of his character from their long association?

During his speech in the Commons debate in June, Sir Lionel Heald, himself a former law officer of the Crown, seemed to be saying that the five Ministers could in no way be blamed for having been deceived by Profumo, since the solicitor Derek Clogg, who was 'about the last man in the world one would choose' to try and deceive had also been deceived. It seemed as though he was claiming that the Ministers of the Crown, who were gathered on this occasion to refute the rumours, had taken a sufficient step in relying on the professional adviser of the man whose good faith was in question. Sir Lionel Heald recalled that on 4 February Mr Clogg, advised by Leading Counsel, had visited the Attorney General and informed him that an approach had been made by someone to Mr Clogg's firm 'which appeared to indicate a demand for money'. Lord Denning looked at this episode to see whether Christine Keeler had committed an offence in asking for money not to publish, and whether her solicitor had behaved correctly. Were there not other aspects that Lord Denning might have asked about? Did he, for example, ask Mr Profumo's solicitors why, believing him innocent, they went to see Christine Keeler who had an article about him ready for the press, the contents of which they neither knew nor apparently tried to discover directly, and then after a little 'to and fro' with her solicitor, said they would ask their client for his instructions on the amount of 'fair recompense' her solicitor suggested should be paid if the article were not published? It is clear from the Denning report that she had no solicitor in this matter until they suggested she should get one.

Lord Denning hardly mentioned the Ward trial. The interpretation of his terms of reference which permitted him to dismiss it in so few words is tenable, although it had at least as much to do with the shape of the Profumo Affair as the sexual rumours about ministers which he so fully and rightly investigated. But many questions remain to worry the public. Was Ronna Ricardo telling the truth when she said she had been threatened by the police into giving false evidence? Why did Vicky Barrett break down when Ward died, confess to a journalist that she too had been lying, and then retract her confession? On whose instructions and with what right had Mandy Rice-Davies been forcibly kept in the country to give evidence against Stephen Ward? And, a question which seems to sum up the others, why did the police find it necessary to interview 140 people before they moved against Stephen Ward? How many people do they usually think it worth interviewing in order to prepare charges of poncing? Is it something like 140? Or is it more like four or five, as common sense would suggest? If they carried out an almost unparalleled operation to get Ward, why did they do so? Who took the decision? How much did it cost? And what made Ward's offences worth it?

It is not right that such questions should remain in our minds after we read such a report on such an Affair. The report was inconclusive, perhaps because to be conclusive would have led to a wholesale condemnation of certain structures of loyalty and complicity which are hard for anyone to see and understand, and especially hard for those who, like the judges, live and work at the heart of the Establishment which sustains those structures.

In the Profumo Affair the political frivolity, the moral myopia, and the herd credulity of latter-day Toryism led to convulsion and the sacrifice of one life, one career, and several reputations. What happened was horrible; it is over, and there is not likely to be more. But we were heading for it; it could hardly not have happened, whether like that or in some similar form. It was the natural fruit of a period of government when convenience was set above justice, loyalty above truth, and appearance above reality.

APPENDIX

HERE are three articles showing how people felt and reacted.
The first is a pessimistic and intuitive French reaction. It is
sensational, and I do not think things were ever consciously
rigged in the direction suggested. But it certainly worked out like
that. The article is by Pierre Accoce, in *Noir et Blanc*, Paris,
August 1963.

Your body, Dr Ward, wrapped in the same grey blanket as when
you were brought into St Stephens Hospital a hundred hours ago, has
been sent to the morgue to await burial.

You never knew about the four-day epilogue which rounded off
your turbulent life. You were in a coma. The surgeons pierced your
body. They stuck it full of tubes, and probes to fight the poison your
blood was carrying round. No go. You knew what you were up to. You
had taken good care to 'disappoint the vultures', as you said in one of
the thirteen notes which made your testament. So your life ended in
the same heavy and mortal sleep as you sank into at your friend Noel
Howard Jones's house, in Chelsea. That was after you had taken a
last consolation, a bottle of Scotch on top of the barbiturates.

That cruel and merciless 'society' in which you had come to believe
(you, so amoral, so sceptical) was going to nail you to a board like a
butterfly. One lady and eleven gentlemen were going to lag you
for seven, as they say in the trade. Seven years prison. Damned
hypocrisy! ... Just because you had apparently introduced one of
your pretty bush-babies to their War Minister in misguided friendship.
And now, to get away from those people, you had sketched a little
pirouette. You killed yourself. Coolly and methodically. But you can't
deny that your suicide had a delightful touch of conditional murder
about it. Society got you, Dr Ward; all those slender little feet shod by
Lilley and Skinner of Oxfort Street [*sic*] finally got the hide off you. You
knew them all right. You knew all their kinks. You knew which of
them liked to be whipped. Your death is bloody convenient for them.
Whatever happens now, even if your last loyalist, Julie Gulliver, stands
up to them and blows a few names, they can breathe freely. Your main
secrets are safe now, in the safest of all bank vaults, your grave. They
can wipe the sweat of fear from under their bowlers, get their chins up,
look at the Rock of Gibraltar and put down a big one, neat. 'No rocks,
my dear; only foreigners put ice in whisky.' You put the fear of

113

God into them, Stephen Ward, and your exit suits them ver
nicely.

We remember your appearance pretty well. You were 'straight
Perhaps not a very desirable acquaintance for some sorts of peopl
but you didn't lie when you were spoken to. It rang true when yo
said you liked life and girls. That's what seems odd today. A ponc
doesn't do away with himself because a court finds him guilty.
lover of life, as you seemed to be, someone breathing pleasure throug
every pore, and getting enough God knows, doesn't do away wit
himself – at least, not without good reason.

Those reasons are inside your skull, and you will never confir
our guesses. But nothing can stop us guessing.

Odd affair. Odd trial. It went off like an arrow, mixing up th
establishment and the dregs, politics and love, espionage and *dolce vit*
Then suddenly, smoke screen ... You were thrown to the wolve
Dr Ward, you and your troop of guides, the Seventh Heaven Troop
delicious Christine, Mandy and Julie, Ronna, Mariella, Ilia, an
tutti quanti i tutti frutti ...

We weren't taken in. We played along. Because that was ho
England wanted it, giving publicity like that to a simple *affaire d
mœurs*, which would have been handled by the lowest courtroom on th
ladder anywhere else in the world. The unexpected new face of ou
neighbour was rather funny, as a matter of fact. She suddenly looke
like us. There was suddenly a sort of rather nice confession. Wel
there we are! Good morning, Mrs England ... You have girls. Yo
have girls. We were amused, and that was all right, because yo
seemed to be playing too, Dr Ward. Your detached manner, you
smiles, your apt answers to Judge Marshall, your conniving winks a
the crowd when you came out of the Old Bailey; all these showed i
Everybody was on the same side. You, us, England. What if Englan
did seem annoyed by the scandalous political overtones of the Profum
Affair, and had the idea of distracting attention by setting the dogs o
you? We were sure their teeth had been filed. We thought you'd file
yours too. . . .

And then you suddenly understood. The teeth were not filed. Yo
were going to get chewed up. You were not going to be acquitte
You were going to carry the whole weight of this scandal alone. O
these scandals; because there were surely lots. You've been done
Dr Ward. They've done you. That's how the secret services find a deco
When a really poisonous affair blows up and compromises the prestig
and the policies of a country, and calls its notables in question, the
have to find a way out. And so, in order to reassure public opinior
they train the spotlight of publicity on a minor aspect of the scandal;

moral affair serves admirably. In exchange for the tarring and feathering, if he agrees, he is promised an acquittal; at the last moment cast-iron evidence will be found to save him. But as a matter of fact, from that very moment, the decoy is lost. He is left abandoned. He is forced. He is left to the hounds. Who cares if he is hurt? If he yells? If he bleeds? So much the better; best of all if he commits suicide. That way he saves the house-killers trouble, if ever he had taken it into his head to shout the truth. . . .

We are wondering, Dr Ward, if your fate was not something like that. Your death reminds us very unpleasantly of those who die for glory, who die that others may live. We thought we were drinking milk during your trial, milk seasoned with rhinoceros-horn powder, a well-known aphrodisiac. But your suicide taught us better. It wasn't milk we were drinking, it was vitriol. And we didn't know. Even before you were buried, the affair boomeranged. One of the prostitutes who laid you low, the girl Barrett, admitted she had been lying. Well, that was belated remorse, and does no good. Because the law says your death closes the case. These terrible useless deaths. . . .

In fifty or sixty years you'll be talked about again; you'll come under the heading of Enigmas of History. It will be asked why you were condemned because the Secretary of State shared one of your girls with a Mr Ivanov, a Soviet naval Attaché. And it will be asked by what miracle the British Government was not blown sky high. . . . They will also inquire into the fate of Mr Michael Eddowes, the London lawyer who on 29 March, two and a half months before the scandal was discovered, alerted the British Security Services because he was surprised (sweet innocent), that Captain Ivanov should have been using their joint mistress to try and get secrets from Mr Profumo, particularly: 'When will nuclear rockets be given to Federal Germany?' Posterity will wonder what Lords Dilhorne and Denning, two important personages of British justice, discovered, and why it was not all published? . . . People will try to find out why the eminent notable, Lord Astor, one of the glories of the United Kingdom, on whose estate occurred some of the most Wardian parties, was never called as a witness at your trial. And perhaps there will be an effort to trace the identity of those powerful men of the kingdom who rode to the sabbath beside you; identities which will have been kept closely secret. . . .

That is what we wish you for your memorial, Dr Ward; that in 2020 the world will find out how it was that a bedroom comedy turned into an Elizabethan drama. Then you can begin to rest in your grave and cease your dissatisfied turning, like the hero of the *Ballad of Reading Gaol*:

> For he who lived more lives than one
> More deaths than one must die.

From Paris to Inverness. Here is part of a leader from the *Highland Herald* of 13 June 1963. A bad smell is a bad smell anywhere.

A page in History

That was a week that was – the one that has just gone, we mean! For it is not often in the reign of a political party's overlordship that we have the ultimate in scandalous gossip and real vice that besets the national morality of a nation. We say now, before the Prime Minister sets about his evasive platitudes and justifications of his sectional interests, that, if we as a nation forget what has been revealed about the Tory hierarchy – including the ... Aims of Industry – during the past fortnight, then we deserve all that happened to the Roman Empire of 2,000 years ago and the Greek and Egyptian Empires before that. Surely, and although we say this with some doubt but nevertheless moral justification, there comes a time when we must say 'this is rotten and corrupt'. For the sake of our children and all that we hold in regard we can no longer uphold the polluted mentality of those who claim 'we are born to lead' – in other words the doubtful spawn of Eton and Harrow, who too often have exercised power in our land. We, funnily enough, are sorry for that aspirant to Scots connexions the Prime Minister, for he is apparently condemned to mix with the kind of society which is now known to keep the company of call-girls and the like – and so is his party. Happy we would be if these implications could be refuted.

Now let us turn to more pleasant and sweet-smelling subjects and escape from the malodorous gossip of the national Press and the political sphere of the past week, to the parochial affairs of our refuse tip at the Longman. For more years than many of us care to remember, the tenants of the Longman housing estate and the Shore area have been subjected to the odour of burning and rotting refuse, dumped blandly at the sea edge of the firth. Fires have broken out and expense has been levied on the ratepayer, but in such a ratio that it was not felt or easily detected by the ratepayer. Only a few hundred people were inconvenienced out of a town's population, so they were easily forgotten. Fair enough! But every dog must have its day. Let this be the day when those who live in the north and east of the town be rid once and for all of the effluvia erupting from the burgh's refuse.

We support wholeheartedly Councillor Wm Smith's suggestion for a refuse-disposal plant that measures up to the demands of this day and age.

In a week when all decent people are appalled and disgusted with the evil and vice which is inherent in and rots our so-called aristocracy, let us get our feet on the ground and in our parish eliminate the same bad taste from our atmosphere by introducing a modern, up-to-date refuse-disposal plant into a progressive town and capital. If we cannot live with the atmosphere of our political bosses, at least let us try to live with our atmosphere as God created it for us.

And lastly a leader, from the *Greenock Telegraph* of 12 June, in which an honest man turns common sense to the semantics of our discontent.

Facts

For once in a way the phrase, 'the true facts', seems to mean something.

Lord Poole, joint chairman of the Conservative Party organization, used it when giving information to the Press about his talk to Tory Party organizers in Newcastle.

What he said of the Profumo affair was: 'The true facts are going to emerge in one form or another in the next few days.'

Of course, in the normal way, to speak of 'true facts' is to be guilty of tautology. Facts would not be facts if they were not true. But in these days there is so much distortion of fact that it is probably necessary to give the guarantee of truth by using the adjective which is already implicit in the noun.

In other words, as far as official statements by politicians are concerned, there are two kind of facts. There is the statement which the speaker hopes will be accepted as true; and there is the statement which is true.

Unfortunately, it has become almost impossible for the innocent listener to decide which is which.

It now appears that four Ministers knew of Mr Profumo's association with the notorious Miss Keeler. They knew of this before he denied in the Commons any impropriety in that association.

Yet they agreed that he should make the official denial.

Can anyone of any experience of the world and its ways be expected to believe that four men, who certainly know a great deal of the world and its ways, would have no suspicion that the 'facts' which Mr Profumo was telling them were not the 'true facts'?

This does appear to be asking rather much of public credulity.

Without being at all cynical and adopting the attitude that 'you never can believe a word these chaps say', we must suggest that if four Cabinet Ministers accept such a statement from a colleague whose way of life must have been pretty well known to them, they lack a quality of common sense which is surely necessary in their important position. . . .

(These three articles are quoted by permission of *Noir et Blanc*, the *Highland Herald*, and the *Greenock Telegraph*.)

*Some more books
published by Penguins
are described on the
following pages*

GREAT BRITAIN OR LITTLE ENGLAND?

John Mander

'Britain has lost an Empire and not yet found a role,' stated Dean Acheson. Was he right?

In this thoughtful and disquieting essay John Mander, whose Penguin Special, *Berlin: Hostage for the West*, was described by the *Guardian* as 'a brilliant book', argues that since the war Britain has never clearly decided whether to be America's chief ally in the Cold War, a mediator between America and Russia, the doyen of an independent Commonwealth, or one more recruit for the European community. Hence so many of our difficulties – the Suez débâcle, impotence during the Cuban crisis, humiliation over the Common Market, hopeless confusion over nuclear armaments.

We face another world today, and John Mander powerfully urges that we should at once re-think our position in it. In the sanest sense his exercise in *real-politik* – terrifying in its precision – is a book about patriotism by a patriot. At a time when old loyalties are dissolving into new, his conclusions are likely to be violently discussed.

VOTERS, PARTIES, AND LEADERS
The Social Fabric of British Politics

Jean Blondel

Are we witnessing the end of class-barriers in the political behaviour of the British voter? Does the businessman vote like the railwayman, the white-collar worker like the unskilled labourer?

Of course they do not. But how different are their voting habits? Trade Unions are Labour-inclined, but all trade unionists are not Labour men. Are these non-Labour trade unionists exceptional? And, at the other end of the scale, are Labour-inclined professional people, managers, and executives rare but interesting exceptions?

These are some of the questions which the newly appointed Professor of Government in the University of Essex attempts to answer in this original book. In examining the background, outlook, and interests of voters, party members, politicians, civil servants, and party leaders, and endeavouring to trace some of the subtle threads that tie certain individuals to certain organizations, he presents an anatomy of the political world. And he asks: 'What is the "Establishment" we talk of? Does it exist? And if so, does it rule?'

THE GENERAL SAYS NO

Britain's Exclusion from Europe

Nora Beloff

When General de Gaulle finally said 'No!', Britain was forced to recognize the duality of her position – in Europe, but not of it. What in fact went wrong?

Throughout the long choppy passage of discussions, negotiations, and backstairs bargains at Brussels and elsewhere, certain 'constants' kept throwing the compass out of the true: de Gaulle's character, Britain's historical and racial links outside Europe, and the past record of British governments over European unity. Daily press reports did not always clarify the larger picture.

Nora Beloff, the *Observer* correspondent, occupied a front seat at the Common Market negotiations. She has used her personal knowledge and understanding of the men involved and of the interests at risk to put together the inside record of the whole, sad fiasco. Here is a story that makes sense. In particular her intuitive reading of de Gaulle's craggy nature and the cold statement she gives of Britain's earlier obstructiveness make the pieces of the Brussels jig-saw slot into position by themselves.

THE OTHER AMERICA

Michael Harrington

In the Affluent Society of the United States there are some fifty million poor Americans. Behind the High Street of prosperity lies 'the other America' – a shadowy district where between 40 and 50,000,000 people struggle to exist below the level of human dignity and decency. Mostly white, these are the unskilled workers, the migrant labourers, the aged, the minorities, the underprivileged members of the affluent society. Maybe they are not actually starving: but they are hungry, and sometimes 'fat with hunger' – such is the effect of cheap foods. Their housing, their education, and their medical care are skimped and inadequate.

First published in the United States this Penguin Special won the 1962 Sidney Hillman Foundation Award and the George Polk Memorial Award for its exposure and analysis of the economic underworld of the richest country on earth. America's is a kind of poverty to which one part of the nation appears to be indifferent or oblivious, whilst the other part – ironically disfranchised to a large extent just because poverty is in a minority today – is coming to endure it as the only American way of life it knows. In a sense such poverty is self-perpetuating. To remove this slur on a great nation, as Michael Harrington emphasizes, will call for a new New Deal, comparable to Roosevelt's pre-war programme.

NOT FOR SALE IN THE U.S.A.

INSIDE RUSSIA TODAY

John Gunther

Authoritative and comprehensive, scrupulously objective and fair minded, Mr Gunther has written a fascinating book in the tradition of his famous 'Inside' studies. The acute observation on the attitudes current in Russia and the wealth of information are vital to any consideration of the present struggle for power and the chances for peace.

'This vast survey of the whole Russian scene is reporting of genius ... A wonderfully balanced and comprehensive survey, free from the two besetting sins of wishful thinking and triviality ... a very remarkable and wonderful book' – Sir David Kelly (formerly H.M. Ambassador to the U.S.S.R.)

'Mr Gunther seems to me unsurpassed in his power first to collect the most important or curious facts about a continent or country, and then to present them with an arresting lucidity. ... This seems to me the most objective and informative book ever written about the U.S.S.R. ... He is extraordinarily sensible' – Raymond Mortimer in the *Sunday Times*

'Very readable ... Gunther's book will do a power of good' – Kingsley Martin in the *New Statesman*

The text of this Penguin edition was fully revised and brought up to date by the author in 1962.

NOT FOR SALE IN THE U.S.A. OR CANADA

A DICTIONARY OF MODERN HISTORY
1789–1945

A. W. Palmer

This book is intended as a reference-companion to the personalities, events, and ideas of the last century and a half. While the prime emphasis is on British affairs and on political topics, the Dictionary is intended to represent trends in the history of all the major regions of the world. Particular care has been taken to include numerous entries on the U.S.A. and on Russia, areas which earlier books tended to neglect. The entries are arranged in alphabetical order (with appropriate cross-references) and are in essay form, ranging in length from little more than 100 words to nearly 2,000. There are entries on economic, social, religious, and scientific developments, but not on the Arts. Explanations are given of some of the famous descriptive phrases of the period. About a third of the entries are biographical.

The book is intended as an aid to study, and not a substitute for it. The author hopes that it will explain the passing allusion and stimulate an interest in unfamiliar facets of historical knowledge.

UNARMED VICTORY

Bertrand Russell

We have recently witnessed an unarmed victory of historic significance. The outcome of the Cuban crisis and of the frontier dispute
between China and India has proved that the greatest powers, even
when they have consolidated a position of strength, may still fight
shy of the irremediable lunacy of modern war. The Russians and the
Chinese voluntarily accepted compromise without loss of face.

In addressing himself directly to Kennedy, Khrushchev, Nehru, and
Chou En-lai, Bertrand Russell valiantly interposed the small voice
of reason during those frightening weeks when we awoke every
morning to the prospect of universal annihilation. In substance his
proposals – as any reader of this Penguin Special can see – were
calculated to achieve exactly what took place. The Russians never
challenged the American blockade of Cuba and the guns were
rested on the Himalayas.

Would it be too sanguine to conclude that the voice of one of the
greatest thinkers of our time was heeded in the chancelleries? At any
rate one reads this account of what one man did when the world was
swaying on the brink of nuclear war with admiration and gratitude.

Also available

NIGHTMARES OF EMINENT PERSONS
SATAN IN THE SUBURBS

Another Penguin by Wayland Young

STRATEGY FOR SURVIVAL

This is a book for clear-minded people tired of hot air who seek a *practical* guide to the desperately urgent problem of nuclear warfare. It is a clarification of the many conflicting policies in the world today. Facts are given which enable readers to form their judgements without prejudice or hysteria.

Wayland Young has realized that confusion of ideas is as dangerous as apathy, and he offers a penetrating analysis of the proposals which have been put forward for reducing the danger of war, showing clearly how far each is likely to succeed. From the conclusions he draws he then goes on to argue the need for a new pattern of international politics and strategy. He urges that Britain should take the initiative in forming a non-nuclear club, in which the countries involved would agree to forgo not only independent but also shared possession of nuclear weapons, and consequently the possibility of using them in war.